THE WAY

Teacher's Book

Second Edition

THE WAY, THE TRUTH & THE LIFE SERIES

By Sr. Marcellina Cooney CP

Editorial Team
Jonathan Bindloss, Angela Grady, Stephen Horsman, Liz McCaul,
Dominic Marshall, Paul Moloney, Rachel Smith and Mary White

Teachers' Enterprise in Religious Education Co. Ltd
Catholic Truth Society

Introduction

The importance of the teacher of Religious Education in our secondary schools cannot be exaggerated. In every respect, it is a challenging task and requires not only knowledge and understanding of the subject but deep faith and conviction as well as a genuine concern for the well being of every student. It is a privileged task that carries enormous responsibility because for many students, the RE teacher is the visible representative of the Catholic Church.

In order to support you, I am very pleased to welcome and introduce this second edition of the Teacher's Book 'The Way' which accompanies the Student's Book and DVD. These form part of the series 'The Way, the Truth & the Life' which has now been published for 3 – 14 year olds.

This programme is based on the Catechism of the Catholic Church and the Religious Education Curriculum Directory for Catholic Schools published by the Bishops' Conference. God calls all people to himself so, in the unit on other faiths, the students will have the opportunity to deepen their understanding of them and will be encouraged to build bonds of friendship with many young people they will come to know.

'The Way' builds on Book 6 of the primary series and ensures continuity and progression. It is possible that not all pupils from primary schools will have used Book 6 so there is a wide range of Power Point presentations, flipcharts for Smart and Promethean interactive whiteboards, audio recordings and worksheets on the DVD to supplement and complement the content of this second edition.

On the DVD, you will also find a great variety of assessment tasks mapped to the Levels of Attainment in Religious Education in Catholic Schools and Colleges, Bishops' Conference Department for Catholic Education and Formation.

The Teacher's and Student's Books and DVD have been produced by the Teachers' Enterprise in Religious Education, that is, by teachers from different parts of the country working in a collaborative manner and pooling their expertise. I thank Fr. Herbert Alphonso SJ most warmly for all the work he has put into the theological notes, the study sessions in Rome and for the great encouragement he continually gives to the teachers involved in the Enterprise.

I trust that all who use this Teacher's Book, Student's Book, DVD and the supporting website www.tere.org will be helped in a clear and direct way in the important task of enabling students to learn about the Catholic faith and to respond to its invitation with growing faith and generosity.

+Vincent Nichols

✝ Vincent Nichols
Archbishop of Westminster

Contents

1. Revelation and Faith

2. God's Promises Fulfilled

3. The Saviour

4. The Church

5. The Sacraments

6. Christianity and Other Faiths

Nihil obstat: Father Anton Cowan (Censor). **Imprimatur:** Rt. Rev. Alan Hopes, V.G., Auxiliary Bishop in Westminster, 18th March 2009, Feast of St. Cyril of Jerusalem. *The* Nihil obstat *and* Imprimatur *are a declaration that the books and contents of the DVD ROM are free from doctrinal or moral error. It is not implied that those who have granted the* Nihil obstat *and the* Imprimatur *agree with the contents, opinions or statements expressed.*

Design, compilation and format Ian Curtis, First Sight Graphics, www.firstsightgraphics.com. **Design and Text copyright** © 2009 Marcellina Cooney CP. Published 2009 by the Teachers' Enterprise in Religious Education Company Limited, 40 Duncan Terrace, London N1 8AL and the Incorporated Catholic Truth Society, 40-46 Harleyford Road, London SE11 5AY. Picture research Marcellina Cooney CP and Ian Curtis.
ISBN 978 1 86082 538 5

Clip art: One Thousand Gospel Images © Jean-Francois Kieffer, Les Presses d'Ile de France

Theological Adviser: Herbert Alphonso SJ
Curriculum Adviser: Joe Fitzpatrick

Acknowledgements
Considerable thanks are due to Liz McCaul, Paul Maloney and Margaret Smart for proof reading 'The Way' Teacher's Book.

Permission credits
Cover photo: stained glass window © CWS Design, 9 Ferguson Drive, Lisburn BT28 2EX. Cover Photo: clouds © Artyfree.
Page 2 Archbishop Vincent Nichols © Peter Jennings.

Methodology

Our starting point in presenting the religious content specified by the Religious Education Curriculum Directory [RECD] is REVELATION. God is always the initiator in the history of our creation and redemption; it is his revealing of himself that makes classroom religious education possible. To begin with, Revelation ensures that we respect the revealed nature of Christian faith.

From Revelation, we move to LIFE IN CHRIST; in other words, we study and reflect on how God makes himself known to us through Jesus, who is truly God and as a man, truly human.

Then we focus on the Church as the People of God and Body of Christ. This leads us to CELEBRATION - the liturgical and sacramental life of the Church, the moral life and the pursuit of holiness.

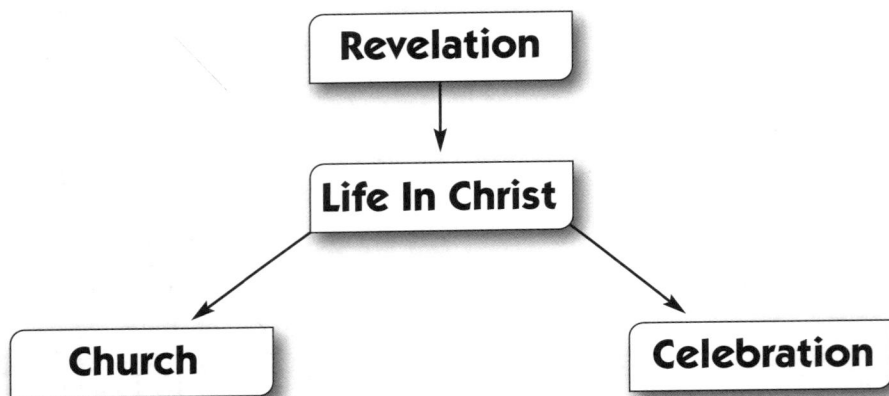

```
                    ┌──────────────┐
                    │  Revelation  │
                    └──────────────┘
                            │
                            ▼
                    ┌──────────────┐
                    │ Life In Christ│
                    └──────────────┘
                      ╱          ╲
                     ▼            ▼
              ┌──────────┐   ┌──────────────┐
              │  Church  │   │  Celebration │
              └──────────┘   └──────────────┘
```

It is essential to make clear connections between the truths of faith and the pupils' own experiences of life. For many, it is only when they see the relevance to their own lives of what they are learning that they become fully engaged in it.

However, the Gospel message always, at some point, takes the person beyond the scope of their own experience, challenging and transforming it. It is a message of a saving and transforming gift.

The syllabus incorporates two **Attainment Targets**:

a) learning **ABOUT** the Catholic Faith (AT1);
b) learning **FROM** the Catholic Faith (AT2).

These are set out in the form of specific key learning objectives for each module.

Overview of Key Stage 3 Syllabus

	Autumn 1	Autumn 2	Spring 1	Spring 2	Summer 1	Summer 2
THE WAY Year 7	Revelation & Faith	God's Promises Fulfilled	The Saviour	The Church	The Sacraments	Christianity & Other Faiths
THE TRUTH Year 8	Creation	Covenant	Mystery of the Eucharist	Paschal Mystery	Prophetic Role of the Church	The Church in Britain
THE LIFE Year 9	Spiritual Quest	Dialogue with Other Faiths	The Gospels	Life in the Spirit	Faith & Culture	Conscience & Morality

Notes For Users

The series *The Way, the Truth & the Life* has been published for 3 – 14 year olds. The text book for Year 7 was the first to be published in 2000. This new edition of *The Way* replaces it.

The contents of this **Teacher's** Book, **Student's** Book and **DVD ROM** are based on the Catechism of the Catholic Church and the Religious Education Curriculum Directory for Catholic Schools, Bishops' Conference of England & Wales, 1996.

The Syllabus for this series incorporates attainment targets: learning *about* the Catholic faith (AT1) and learning *from* the Catholic faith (AT2). These are set out in the form of specific key learning objectives for each module.

The **DVD ROM** to support *The Way* offers an extensive variety of resources: Power Point Presentations; flipcharts for interactive whiteboards (Smart and Promethean); together with creative worksheets to stimulate and motivate all abilities.

There is a Power Point presentation on 'Assessment for Learning' for training teachers and a wide range of assessment tasks mapped to the Levels of Attainment in Religious Education in Catholic Schools and Colleges, Bishops' Conference publication, 2007.

This **DVD ROM** is published by the Teachers' Enterprise in Religious Education Company Limited; details can be found on the supporting website www.tere.org

KEY to symbols and abbreviations in this Teacher's Book:

WS (with a number) = Worksheet on the DVD ROM

PPP = Power Point Presentation on the DVD ROM

IWB = Flipcharts for Promethean and/or Smart interactive whiteboards on the DVD ROM

Audio recording on the DVD ROM

Reflective activity or prayer

CCC = Catechism of the Catholic Church

RECD = Religious Education Curriculum Directory, Bishops' Conference of England and Wales

IWB = Interactive whiteboard

Tips For Teaching & Learning

Starters:

As pupils enter the classroom have something for them to do right away.
- Write down the key learning objective (KLO).
- Ask probing questions to find out what they already know about the KLO. Demand more than superficial answers.
- Remember it helps to start with a question rather than a statement.
- Recap on the previous lesson by asking a series of probing questions.
- Pupils record new words and their meaning.
- Use new words to make sentences to show the meaning.
- Play 'Lucky dip': a pupil picks a key word out of a box; then has to explain that word and what they know about it.
- Or 'Just a minute': a pupil selects a word from the board and talks about it for a minute.
- Or 'Guess my word': a pupil picks a word out of a box and talks about it without saying the word. The rest of the group guess the word as quickly as possible.
- Quick quiz: Pupils stand behind their chairs for a quick quiz on key words and only sit down when they have given the correct answer.

Pupils need to feel they are being challenged and kept on the alert.

Purpose & Relevance:

The main part of the lesson is introduced by the teacher telling the pupils what they are going to learn, rather than what they are going to do. Lessons have focus. Pupils need to perceive a purpose and relevance in what they are doing. It will help if they have a copy of the Key Learning Objectives in their exercise books and are able to tick them off as soon as they have been achieved.

Another feature is active teaching. For example, the teacher will demonstrate but at the same time involve pupils by constantly asking probing questions. The brain functions best when it is engaged in a constant variety of activities rather than passively absorbing information.

Frequently ask pupils to stop, think, suggest and explain. They might have a moment to talk to a partner, bounce ideas off each other and come up with suggestions. The teacher facilitates the process rather than directs the entire sequence.

A key feature is asking pupils to explain their thinking or working out. Invite pupils to come to the front of the class to do so. It is helpful to highlight good ways of working and show how good learners operate. Encourage them to take responsibility for their own learning.

Importance of Reflection:

Reflection is crucial to the learning process. It helps pupils to see the relevance of what they are learning for their own lives or the lives of others. Encourage them to make links with their daily lives in school, at home or the area in which they live.

Plenaries

The lesson closes with a plenary session in which the teacher draws out the key points. Pupils do most of the work. They are encouraged to explain what they have learned and how it can be used. Regular homework helps individuals to consolidate what they have learnt in the lesson or to prepare for the next one.

The final plenary is an opportunity to round off, summarise the lesson and underline what has been learnt. It helps pupils to focus on the most important rather the most recent points, what they have learned and the progress they have made. It should aim to refocus pupils on the objectives that have featured in the lesson. It is also a time to look back and look forward, and to relate work in the lesson to real life situations.

Plenaries are also useful part way through a lesson: a moment to pause when the teacher draws the class together, checks understanding and directs the class to the next phase of work.

Plenaries will vary in length, two minutes on one day, twenty minutes on another, depending on the style and format of what the teacher has planned. To provide the necessary variety, they can be used to:

- draw together what has been learnt, to highlight the most important rather than the most recent points, to summarise key facts, ideas and vocabulary, and stress what needs to be remembered;

- question pupils and rectify any remaining misunderstandings;

- make links to other work and what the class will go on to do next;

- highlight the progress pupils have made and remind them about their personal targets;

- set homework to extend or consolidate class work and prepare for future lessons.

In drawing the lesson together, the vital part is helping pupils to think about what they may have learnt by getting them to summarise the ideas in the lesson.

Ultimately learning should be an adventure with a sense of enjoyment. If lessons have meaning and purpose for the lives of the pupils they will want to be involved.

Teachers should set high expectations for themselves, live up to them and then encourage the pupils to do the same.

Assessment for Learning:

In preparation for teaching each module, it is best to have chosen an assessment task from the Folder 'Assessment tasks & levels' in advance. This should not be an 'end of module test' but used as a classroom activity that will be marked in depth and awarded a 'level of attainment'.

DVD ROM: PPP 'Assessment for Learning'

DVD ROM: PPP 'Exemplification work from Years 5 & 6 and Word documents.
This exemplification material is from Primary schools using 'The Way, the Truth & the Life' series. It is intended to give teachers an idea of the high quality work that a significant number of pupils in Years 5 & 6 are capable of producing.

Contents of DVD ROM

Introduction

Archbishop Vincent Nichols

Notes for users

Overview of Key Stage 3 Syllabus

Syllabus 'The Way'

Theology of the Bible

Notes on Original Sin

7.1 Revelation & Faith Power Points (PPP)

1. The Bible
2. How to use the Bible
3. Looking for Bible reference
4. Starter: Getting to know a person
5. Glory of God
6. Abraham's Faith
7. Sarah hears God's promise
8. Abraham's Faith is tested
9. David's Brothers
10. David Repents

Worksheets

WS 1   Bible worksheet for PPP
WS 2   Bible worksheet with answers to PPP
WS 3   Bible – finding your way
        (for less able)
WS 4   Big Questions
WS 5   Faith Journey
WS 6   Faith Journey (for less able pupils)
WS 7   Faith, Challenge, Blessing chart
WS 8   Role-play: Abraham & Reporter
WS 9   Sarah's Faith
WS 10   Sarah's Diary
WS 11   Abraham, Man of Faith or Fool
(writing frame for less able & 11a for more able pupils)
WS 12   David & Goliath – story (for less able)
WS 13   David's Conscience
WS 14   David: Temptations Versus Conscience
WS 15   David Repents
WS 16   Final Plenary

Other Resources

Map & notes

Flip Charts For Promethean & Smart

The Bible
Revelation & Faith
Abraham
Abraham's faith is tested (2)
David
David's downfall
Solomon
Notes on Flipcharts

Assessment

Twenty-two assessment Tasks and Levels
Assessment sheets:
- Abraham's Faith is challenged
- Is Abraham a man of faith or a fool?
- David: temptations versus conscience
- David & the prophet Nathan
- "Temptations are not bad in themselves"

7.2 God's Promises Fulfilled Power Points

1. Reasons for Exile
2. Exiles longing for God
3. Suffering Servant prophecies
4. Moses
5. Zechariah's prophecy
6. God's Promises Fulfilled - Nativity

Worksheets

WS 1   Exile: reasons, effects
WS 2   Ruvinbo's experince
WS 3   Bridge between OT and NT
WS 4   Mary's Song (for less able pupils)
WS 5   Mary's Magnificat – bubble map
WS 6   Scripture through Art: Nativity
WS 7   Fulfilment of God's plan in the Nativity
        – Final Plenary
WS 8   Christmas cards
WS 9   St. Joseph (for less able pupils)

Other Resources

7.2   Divided Kingdoms overview
7.2   Drama – Shepherds (for less able pupils)
7.2   Innkeeper's wife reflects: script &
       – audio recording for reflection
7.2   Circle Time: Mary reflects

Flipcharts For Promethean & Smart

Exile (1)
Exile (2)
Mary & Joseph
Zechariah's Prophecy
Reflection on Mary (1)
Birth of Jesus
Notes on Flipcharts

Assessment

Sixteen Assessment Tasks and Levels
Assessment sheets:
- Exile – freedom to return
- Servant Songs
- Mary's Prophecy
- Fulfilment of God's plan (Guided Thinking)

7.3   The Saviour
Power Point Presentations
1. Starter: John the Baptist
2. Beatitudes
3. Jesus true God and true man
4. Moses (7.2 repeated)
5. Son of the widow of Nain
6. The Vine

Worksheets
WS 1   John the Baptist
WS 2   Adulterous Woman
WS 3   Jesus visits his home town (for more able)
WS 4   Private Eye – writing frame (for less able)
WS 5   Jesus true, God and true man (for less able)
WS 6   Mystery of the Incarnation
WS 7   Living out the teaching of Jesus (less able)
WS 8   Invitation to the Kingdom
WS 9   Jesus is the Way, the Truth & the Life
WS 10   Final plenary

Other Resources
7.3   Values A Values B
7.3   Beatitudes
7.3   Dining with the Pharisees
7.3   Poem: Mystery of Jesus + audio recording
7.3   Picture of Jesus, Divine Mercy
7.3   Cure of sick man at pool
7.3   Cure of Centurion's servant

Flipcharts For Promethean & Smart
Values
Mission of Jesus
Jesus human & divine
Who is Jesus for us?
St. John Vianney
Notes on Flipcharts

Assessment

Seventeen assessment Tasks & Levels
Assessment Sheets:
- John the Baptist's Advice
- John the Baptist tasks
- Beatitudes (Guided Thinking)
- The Beatitudes & Your Values (Guided Thinking)
- Tasks on Jesus
- Mystery of the Incarnation
- Jesus & the Religious Authorities (Guided Thinking)
- Mystery of the Incarnation (for more able)

7.4   The Church
Power Point Presentations
1. Disciples - starter
2. Peter – profile
3. Conversion of Saul
4. Catacombs
5. Priests' Hiding Holes
6. Early Christians Martyrs
7. Death of the Apostles
8. Paul's martyrdom
9. China: The Torch of Faith
10. Inside a church

Worksheets
WS 1   (1) Research task
WS 2   Peter – character analysis
WS 3   Apostles overwhelmed by events
WS 4   Early Christian community – bubble map
WS 5   Stephen's speech - timeline
WS 6   Paul – inquiry brief
WS 7   Peter & Paul (for less able)
WS 8   People of God = Church (for less able)
WS 9   Handing Over – what does it mean?
WS 10   Why did Christianity spread so quickly?
WS 11   Quick Quiz
WS 12   Island Game
WS 13   Project on parish church
WS 14   Youth of the Church (for less able)
WS 15   Ordination of bishop – notes and task

Other Resources
7.4   "Do you love me" - audio recording
7.4   Stephen's speech
7.4   Overview Creation to Church
7.4   Map of Paul's Journeys
7.4   Church in China: commentary for PPP

Flipcharts For Promethean & Smart
Disciples
Birth of Church & key words
Drama unfolds
Church as People of God
Notes on Flipcharts

Assessment
Fourteen Assessment Tasks & Levels
Assessment Sheets:
- Drama unfolded (Guided Thinking)
- Early Christians and Christians today (Guided Thinking)
- Saul's conversion – based on picture in Student's Book page 69.
- Ship of Peter (for more able pupils)

7.5   The Sacraments
Power Point Presentations
1. Introduction to signs & symbols
2. Baptism by immersion
3. Sacraments of Initiation
4. Sacraments: symbolic actions
5. Pope Benedict XVI : Reconciliation
6. Prodigal Son
7. Sacrament of Confirmation

Worksheets
WS 1   Effects of the Sacraments
WS 2   Tuning In
WS 3   Sacraments linked to Life
WS 4   Sacraments linked to Eucharist
WS 5   Baptism - Signs & symbols (for less able)
WS 6   My Baptism – What happened (for less able)
WS 7   My Baptism Record (for less able)
WS 8   Baptism of Jesus (Extension for more able)
WS 9   The way back
WS 10   Gifts sin damages (for less able)
WS 11   Steps to recovery for us
WS 12   Miracles
WS 13   Reflect on the Sacraments

7.5 Other Resources
Opening our hearts - guided meditation

Flipcharts For Promethean & Smart
Original Sin
Physical & spiritual needs
Sacraments
Sacraments linked to life
Prodigal Son
Notes on Flipcharts

Assessment
Seventeen Assessment Tasks & Levels
Assessment Sheets:
- Sacraments/Prayer/Action
- Prodigal Son & Steps to Recovery
- Sacrament of Reconciliation
- Sacrament of the Sick

7.6   Christianity & Other Faiths
Power Points
1. Starter – St. Paul
2. St. Francis Xavier
3. Edel Quinn
4. Annalena Tonelli
5. Pope John Paul II and the Jews
6. World Faiths: Beliefs
7. World Faiths: Worship & Behaviour

Worksheets
WS 1   Apostles overwhelmed by events
WS 2   Countries with a Catholic majority
WS 3   St. Francis Xavier: Questions for group discussion
WS 4   St. Francis Xavier
WS 5   Edel Quinn time-line
WS 6   Gladys Aylward – faith, challenge, blessing
WS 7   Missionaries I admire (for less able)
WS 8   How missionaries affect others
WS 9   KWL chart
WS 10   Other Faiths – Values we share
WS 11   Jewish worship (for less able pupils)
WS 12   Annalena Tonelli

7.6 Other Resources
Edel Quinn biography
Gladys Aylward biography
World Religions statistics
World Religions pie charts
Annalena Tonelli

Flipcharts For Promethean & Smart
Christianity, St. Paul,
St. Francis Xavier
Notes on Flipcharts

Assessment
Seven Assessment Tasks & Levels
Assessment Sheets:
- St. Paul
- Values We Share (Guided Thinking)
- Other Faiths

Note: This DVD ROM has been developed for teachers, by teachers working on a voluntary basis. It is illegal to copy this disc for another school and should you do so you will not only be breaking the law but you will also be depriving your colleagues of income necessary to develop further resources.

1. Revelation & Faith

Religious Education Curriculum Directory
"The Scriptures are the living Word of God, written under the guidance of the Holy Spirit, received and faithfully handed on within the living Tradition and teaching of the Church" (page 14).

Catechism of the Catholic Church
"In order to gather together scattered humanity God calls Abram from his country, his kindred and his father's house, and makes him Abraham, that is, 'the father of a multitude of nations'. 'In you all the nations of the earth shall be blessed,'" (Catechism of the Catholic Church para. 59)

Key Learning Objectives:

Attainment Target 1: Learning *about* the Catholic faith.
Attainment Target 2: Learning *from* the Catholic faith.

- Understand what the Bible is *(On the DVD)*.

- Reflect on who God is and how he makes himself known to us.

- Reflect on how Abraham's journey of faith in God began.
  o Think about our relationship with God.

- Understand that God made a covenant with Abraham and through him with us.
  o Reflect on what this means for us.

- Know that when God asked Abraham to sacrifice his only son, he was testing his faith.
  o Reflect on the meaning of this story for us.

- Understand that David was chosen by God to be a great leader.
  o Reflect on David's response to God's call and our own response.

- Know about David's downfall.
  o Reflect on what this tells us about human nature.

- Reflect on how God kept his covenant with David and will keep his promises with us.

Theological Notes

1 Revelation and Faith

When we think of "Revelation" we immediately have an image of a *body of truths* which God has communicated to us, so that "Faith" then becomes our accepting and believing in this *whole body of* truths. This image - usually formed and fostered in our formative years as Christians and Catholics - can unfortunately be so completely abstract that it totally deprives both "Revelation" and "Faith" of their intensely *personal* – indeed, *interpersonal* – character and content. **"God is LOVE"** (1 Jn. 4:8, 16) and, as LOVE, God communicates and hands over himself to us. In other words, God hands over his own life and love, with his power of living and loving, to us. **This is, at its very heart, what we call REVELATION.** <u>As a consequence</u>, of course, what is offered us by God is a "body of truths" concerning who he is, what his love has planned for us, and how we can best know him, love him, and obtain what he has, in his love, designed for each and all of us.

Because God **loves** each and all of us very personally, he does not impose himself on us nor force us to accept his handing over of himself, his life and love, to us. He has created us as *"free"* human beings; he respects our freedom. Of course, God invites and attracts – even solicits – our personal freedom to accept his offer because, in his love for us, he knows that such an acceptance of his plan and design will make us genuinely and truly happy. So, then, **our active and free opening of our hearts and selves to receive God's gift and communication of himself, his life and his love to us is, at its very heart, what we call FAITH.** Again, <u>as a consequence</u>, such FAITH entails freely accepting, and believing in, all the truths which God has shared with us concerning who he is, what he has planned for us, and how we can best know him, love him and obtain what, in his love, he has designed for each and all of us.

....

While it is true that we can, by means of our natural powers of reasoning, come to know God's existence and some of his qualities or attributes with certainty through encountering, and reflecting on, the works of God that surround us in creation (i.e. by way of *natural* theology), there exists a wholly 'other' level or sphere of knowledge of God which human beings cannot reach through their powers and resources of reasoning; **this** is the proper domain of **divine Revelation**. In freedom and love God communicates himself to human beings, unveiling his own ineffable mystery through making known his eternal plan and design of saving all humanity – indeed, the entire universe – in and through his Son Jesus Christ. God reveals this design of his in its fullness by sending his Son as true Man among us to make known and carry out his plan in the power of the Holy Spirit of love.

In a nutshell, God's plan can be summed up as follows: God wants to communicate his own divine life and love to all men and women, to make them his own – real, even if "adopted" – sons and daughters in His one and only Son, Jesus Christ. In thus revealing himself and his plan, God wishes to make us capable of freely responding, beyond our own natural resources, to his will and design of our knowing and loving him, to the point of sharing, in his Son Jesus, his own divine life and love.

From all the above, it becomes plain that if "REVELATION" is a wholly free gift of God to us, so too is "FAITH" inasmuch as God makes us human beings capable of freely responding, beyond our merely human resources, to His plan and design of love for us. It is also plain that "REVELATION" and "FAITH" are intimately "correlative"- God's freely-gifted communication of himself and his plan of love calls for human beings' free collaboration in accepting and living out this plan.

This divine, eternal plan and design God carries out in human history gradually and *pedagogically* through words, actions and events made known, step by step, in the biblical narrative, culminating as it does in the Person and salvific mission of his beloved Son Jesus Christ – words, actions and events which mark the various historical stages of divine revelation.

....

From the start, God revealed himself to our first parents Adam and Eve, as the Book of Genesis tells us; he invited them to an intimate communion with himself, clothing them with the splendid dignity of original grace and justice. Even when they disobeyed God and, through sin, lost their friendship with God, he did not abandon our first parents to the powers of death; soon after their fall he promised the Redeemer, and took personal care of them and their offspring. Again and again he offered a covenant to human beings, and through the prophets taught them to hope for salvation.

Thus, when the unity of the human race was threatened and began to be destroyed by sin, God sought in every way to save humankind in his love. After the deluge God made an alliance with Noah to express his will to save "all nations". Even so, the pride and arrogance of selfish humanity concurred, through the construction of the Tower of Babel, to build its own kind of unity in opposition to, and frustration of, God's loving plan and design. But God's faithful love relentlessly pursued the pedagogical carrying out of his design of love; to bring together into unity the human race divided and dispersed through the sinful pride and selfishness of humankind. God chose Abraham, calling him out of his own country, his father's house and parentage, to make of him "the father of a multitude of peoples", in whom all the nations of the earth would be blessed. This alliance which God made with Abraham and confirmed with his descendants Isaac and Jacob – the Patriarchs, as all three are called – would make of the people descending from them the depository of the promises made to these patriarchs; this people would be known as "the people of the election", that is, "the chosen people", called by God to prepare the reassembling one day in the unity of the Church all the scattered children of God, brought together as one family by the redeeming work and mission of Jesus Christ.

In this wondrous pedagogical manner of faithfully carrying out his loving design, God made of Abraham and his descendants a people to whom he revealed his Law through Moses. He patiently got ready this, his chosen, people, right through the period of the Kings – especially King David, the King after God's own heart – and that of the prophets, to welcome the salvation he had planned, in love, for all humanity.

Indeed, God revealed himself finally, fully and definitively through and in his Son Jesus Christ, in whom he sealed his final alliance for all time. Jesus Christ is the final and definitive word of God the Father: in **him** all God's revelation is completely contained and summed up, so that, after him, there is and will be no further revelation (cf. Heb. 1:1-2).

Herbert Alphonso SJ

Additional Suggestions and Resources

Understand what the Bible is. (See DVD)

NOTE:

Pupils from Primary schools using 'The Way, the Truth & the Life' (WTL) will have covered a module on the Bible in Year 4 and should be familiar with looking up references. An outline of the Key Stage 2 syllabus can be found on www.tere.org

It is important for teachers to remember that Year 7 will have had six years of religious education so it is best not to underestimate what they already know and can do. It is advisable to start this module as quickly as possible in the first term because there is a lot to cover and an effort has been made where possible, to tie in with the liturgical year.

Remember it is much more important to get into the spirituality of the scriptures than to accumulate facts.

The DVD 'THE WAY' is available from the Teachers' Enterprise in Religious Education, 40 Duncan Terrace, Islington, London N1 8AL, telephone 020 7359 2642, www.tere.org Publications.

[Note: In the Assessment Folder on the DVD for this module there are approximately twenty assessment tasks and some assessment sheets mapped to the Bishops' Conference Levels of Attainment in RE. It will help if you plan which assessment task(s) best suits your pupils before you start to teach the module. See Power Point presentation on **ASSESSMENT FOR LEARNING** *in the* **ASSESSMENT FOLDER***.*

Starting point: (if pupils have little knowledge of the Bible)
What is the Bible? Ask the pupils what they think the Bible is? What stories do they already know? What is their favourite story? Why?

PPP The Bible: Recap by showing the Power Point presentation on what the Bible is.

WS1 worksheet to accompany PPP.
WS 2 worksheet with answers to the PPP.

Explain that in this half term we are going to focus on the Old Testament. Imagine what it was like for the people who had no understanding of what God is like. It was only with the coming of Jesus that we have been able to really grasp the depth of the love of God for us. But in Old Testament times God revealed himself little by little.

PPP Looking up a Bible reference.

PPP How to use the Bible.

Bible Quiz (for less able pupils).

Additional worksheets:

www.tere.org go to Secondary, click on KS3 Support Material: 'Bible Library'; 'Bible Overview'; 'Bible Types NT'; 'Bible Types OT'.

www.tere.org go to WTL Support Material: 'God Speaks to us in the Bible'; 'The Bible is the Word of God'.

FLIPCHARTS IWB 'The Bible'.

Reflect on who God is and how He makes Himself known to us.

---

*[**Note:** In an attempt to simplify the text in the Student's Book Abram's name is called Abraham. In Genesis 17:5 God changed Abram's name to Abraham because he was making him father of many nations].*

PPP 'Getting to know people': Starting point: Think of how we get to know people. How do we learn to trust them? How well can we get to know them? Does it take time?

Explain: Each person finds God or God finds them in a unique way that is special to them. A starting point for many is the beauty and order of the universe. We have only to take time to study its beauty to be led to the belief that it must have a designer. Watching the sunrise or sunset can be a deeply spiritual experience as the Psalmist says, 'The heavens proclaim the glory of God' (Ps. 18).

PPP: 'The Glory of God' use as a silent meditation. You may wish to play very soft music while watching it. This PPP should help pupils to observe the beauty of God's creation and prepare the way for our real starting point: REVELATION and FAITH.

Explain to pupils that they are now going to learn a new way of thinking about what they learn in RE – it is called theology. They will have to think in a deeper way and look for meanings that are not immediately obvious.

Faith

Faith is like absolutely trusting what someone says is true even though there is no proof. We generally say we have faith in someone when we trust and have confidence in them. But faith in God is a supernatural gift.

Explain: the difference between revelation, to reveal something of ourselves to others and **Divine Revelation.**

Divine Revelation is God's own 'unveiling' or revealing of God and God's plan for us. It is a gift from God. It gives us a share in God's **divine knowledge**. It prepares us to share in God's **divine life**. We are going to see how this plan unfolds in the life of Abraham who, because of his **absolute trust** in God, is known as our father in faith.

Discuss: Why do you think that the writer has put Revelation and Faith together?
· Help pupils to understand that God will only reveal Himself to those who have faith. **Revelation calls for a response in faith**.
· Step by step, God gradually unfolds His plan to people who have absolute faith and trust in Him.

Why do you think Abraham's faith needed to be educated and challenged?
· God had great plans for Abraham but He had to be sure that Abraham was ready to respond in faith to each challenge God sent. In this way, Abraham's faith grew.
· It is a little bit like a parent starting to give a child tasks to do. The more reliable the child became the more the parents would give him/her responsibility.

Flipcharts: Revelation & Faith

Additional activities
WS 4 'Big Questions': this could be used as a 'starter'.

WS 5 'Faith Journey' this could be used as a meditation and also as an activity to help pupils to focus on their own faith journey. It is also a preparation for the next Key Learning Objective [KLO].

> **Reflect on how Abraham's journey of faith in God began.**
> **Think about our relationship with God.**

Starting point: Invite pupils to think of their faith journey. Were there difficulties along the way? Was it difficult to trust God? Where did they find help? What can they do to strengthen their faith? Do they know of any inspirational people whose example strengthens their faith?

WS 6: 'Faith Journey' (for less able pupils). This could also be used for a starter as it will help to focus the pupils' minds.

Explain:

- Little by little, God was helping Abraham to know the part God was playing in his life.
- Abraham had to come to an understanding of ONE GOD – rather than the polytheistic concept of many gods. This was a totally new concept because belief in polytheism was widespread at that time.
- God challenged Abraham so that his faith would grow.
- God's promises were realised in the distant future so they required great faith on Abraham's part.

Examples:

- God took the initiative; He acted first.
- God broke into Abraham's life and said: "Leave your country and your kindred (relations) and your father's house and go to the land that I will show you" (Gen. 12:1).
- I am giving you no details, God seems to say; I am not telling you for how long, or what kind of people you will meet.
- In faith, Abraham left and did as God had asked him.
- Abraham made the complete act of faith: always putting his trust in God.
- God comes back to educate and challenge Abraham's faith over and over again.
- Each time Abraham's relationship with God grows stronger and God is able to give him extraordinary blessings.

Additional activities

Start to build up KEY WORDS, pupils learn their meaning and then play 'Just a minute': a pupil picks a key word from a box and explains the meaning of it within one minute.

PPP 'Abraham's Faith'

WS 7 'FAITH, CHALLENGE, BLESSINGS' from the Pupil's Book page 4.

Flipcharts: Abraham.

Reflection: Take a few moments in silence to think of a time when your faith in God was tested. Talk to God in your heart and then write some of your thoughts. *[Let the pupils know that if they wish to keep their thoughts private they could put them in an envelope and seal it. This is not a piece of work to be marked].*

For a simplified overview of Salvation History, type into Google 'God's Story: Christian answers.net'.

Understand that God made a covenant with Abraham and through him with us. Reflect on what this means for us.

Starting point: Ask pupils to give examples to show the difference between promises we frequently make and what they would consider to be a very solemn promise.

Explain: A solemn promise between two people or groups of people is called a **'Covenant'**. The covenant is made when the people accept it and they undertake to fulfil their part of it. For example, when a man and a woman get married, they solemnly promise to love each other completely for the rest of their lives. For His part, God promises to be faithful to the married couple and give them the help they need. This is His Covenant with them.

God made a COVENANT with Abraham: see **Pupil's Book** page 8.
It was at this time that God changed Abram's name to Abraham. The name Abraham means 'Father of a great multitude of nations'. The name of Abraham's wife was also changed from Sarai to Sarah, which means 'princess', probably to mark the end of her barrenness in the promise that she was to have a child.

Additional Activities
WS 8 Role-play: Abraham & the Reporter.

Imagine you are Sarah. Retell the story from your point of view and include the questions you would have wanted to ask Abraham. Use the following texts from Genesis to guide you:

12: 1-9	The call of Abraham; God's promise of the land; what the journey was like
17: 1-8	The Covenant and Abraham's response
17: 15-19	The promise of a baby; the start of a new nation
21: 1-7	The birth of Isaac

PPP 'Sarah hears God's promise

WS 9 'Sarah's Faith'.

Work in pairs. Discuss: What was the biggest challenge that Abraham and Sarah now had to face? Think of their age and the oldest people you know.

> **Know that when God asked Abraham to sacrifice his only son, He was testing his faith.**

Note: At that time, human beings were sacrificed to pagan deities, such as the gods and goddesses of fields, rivers, woods and hills, for many motives, such as ensuring a good harvest for the following year.

Explain: A good teacher observes the progress a pupil makes and seeks ways to set more challenging tasks in order to increase the person's knowledge and understanding of the subject. A good parent gradually gives more responsibility to a child to help him/her to mature. God wants each one of us to grow in our faith and trust in Him, so life is not going to be easy and comfortable – there will be challenges. It is easy to thank God when everything works out according to our plans. But when our hopes are dashed – that's when we have to stop and think: what we want may not be what God wants for us. In the long run, God always wants what is best for us, but we can only see the here and now.

Share examples: Try to give an example from your own life and invite pupils to share any experiences they have had.

Make links with Abraham's experience:
- God promised Abraham a son. Isaac was born.
- God promised Abraham many descendants, so Isaac was going to have many children.
- Then God asks Abraham to offer his son as a burnt offering to Him.
- Has God forgotten His promise? Is He a cruel God that would ask a father to sacrifice his son?
- Remember God made a covenant, a very solemn promise with Abraham. He promised Abraham that he would be the father of many nations.
- God had not gone back on His word. God wanted Abraham's faith to grow so that He could give him many blessings.

PPP Abraham's faith is tested

Flipchart: Abraham's faith is tested

Make further links:
Because of Abraham's great faith in God he is remembered in Eucharistic Prayer 1 of the Mass

as 'our father in faith'. "Father, look with favour on these offerings and accept them as once you accepted the sacrifice … of Abraham, our father in faith …."

The ram caught in the bush was God's gift to Abraham so that he did not have to give up his son, Isaac. We now know that God gave up His only Son, Jesus, to be the sacrifice that takes away our sins. When we come to study the Mass we will understand that this is the gift that shows God's tremendous love for us.

WS 10 Sarah's Diary.

Activity Pupil's Book page 11 HOT SEAT
The teacher picks three pupils to be in the 'hot seat'.
The rest of the class asks these pupils questions.

Assessment Folder
Assessment sheet: **Abraham's faith is challenged**

Assessment sheet: **Is Abraham a man of faith or a fool?** (With points to consider).
WS 11 If you want to use this as a classroom or homework activity see worksheet 11 for a writing frame for the less able and worksheet11a for the more able pupils.

Abraham Foolish

He leaves a good home.
He is well-respected in the city.
He is well-off.
He has waited a long time for a son whom he is willing to sacrifice.
Sarah is too old to have children.

Abraham Faith Filled

Believes in ONE God while his neighbours believe in many gods.
He leaves his home.
He leaves his family.
He leaves his country.
He uproots his family.
He is ready to sacrifice his only son – the son that God promised to him.

Additional worksheets:
See www.tere.org KS3 Support Material: 'Abraham Isaac Sacrifice' and for more able pupils 'Abraham, Isaac & Jesus' Sacrifice'.

Prayer:
Lord, I want to thank you for all you have given to me. I ask you for the grace to be able to trust in you at all times. May I be able to welcome you into my life daily and trust that you know what is best for me! Amen.

Know that David was chosen by God to be a great leader.

Starting Point: Discuss what people look for when they want to choose leaders?

Share: Ask pupils what they already know about David. Listen to see if they will say anything about his brothers and make a note of it. Set the scene: everyone knew a great prophet was coming. David knew he was not invited to be there, he was left to look after the sheep. He could have been resentful and said to himself: 'They look down on me because I am the youngest. They will not even let me see the prophet." Instead, David gets on with whatever he is asked to do and believes that God will take care of him.

Pause: How do we feel when we have been overlooked or considered too young for something?

Read: 'David is chosen' from the Pupil's Book. Invite questions and comments on text.

Flipcharts: David Is Chosen.

PPP: David's brothers.
What do they think God was teaching the brothers? What can we learn from it?

Story of **David & Goliath** as told by one of the soldiers (for less able pupils).

WS 12 David & Goliath: David knows what he can do and what he cannot do. He has the courage to be himself. He knew that the only power he had was God's power in him. He completely trusted in God to work through him.

Reflect: There is always a temptation for us not to be ourselves but to imitate successful people. How often do we want to have the latest fashion, to copy pop singers, footballers, etc. Sometimes, we want to do everything and concentrate on everything material and we miss the opportunities we could seize to be alone with God.

Prayer:
Dear Jesus,
Help me to know myself. Help me to value the real gifts you have given to me. Help me not to be led astray with false ambitions. May I remember to make time to truly get to know your will for me. Amen.

Starting Point: Give an example of a temptation, such as, *'I am tempted to sit down and let all of you chat for this lesson. If I did this – I could rest but you would be falling behind in your work.'*

a) Ask the pupils to identify the possible consequences of your temptation.

b) Ask pupils to give another example of a temptation and consequences.

c) Explain that in this section we will be looking at an example of a true and very real temptation that King David succumbed to and the consequences it had for several people.

Flipcharts: Starter.

Flipcharts: David's success. Recap:

- Who chose David? *(God chose him.)*
- Who gave David the strength and courage to challenge Goliath?
  (God gave him incredible strength and made him one of the greatest kings in the history of his people.)
- Do you think David was aware of the great gifts he had received from God? Why?
- Temptations can come when we least expect them. David had become complacent – what do you think happened? Why? Read the Pupil's Book.

David's downfall – What does it teach us?

- Faith and trust need to be fed and sustained by prayer or they will grow weak.
- Power can corrupt – it can make you rely on your own strength and not on God's.
- Power can make you selfish – it could make you believe you have a right to things to which you do not have a right.
- People sometimes try to cover up what they have done wrong instead of taking responsibility for their actions in front of God and others. This can lead to more unhappiness.
- People sometimes ignore what will make them truly happy – i.e. loving others and acting justly. Instead they will take routes to a superficial type of happiness.

Activities
WS 13: 'David's conscience'.

WS 14: David - 'Temptations versus conscience'.

Assessment Folder assessment sheet: **'David and the prophet Nathan'** (Double bubble thinking map).

Assessment Folder assessment sheet: **'Temptations are often not bad in themselves'**.

    a) Can you think of examples where this is true?

    b) Can you think of any examples when it is not true?

(Example for a): If you overcome the temptation to steal something that belongs to another person, you strengthen your own character and become a trustworthy person.

(Example for b): A temptation is bad when we give in to it. This may mean that we commit a sin – for example, we notice that someone has dropped some money without being aware of it. We pick it up and put it in our own pocket without telling the person. That means we have stolen it.

It is essential for pupils to see this PPP because it emphasises God's mercy and forgiveness for all who repent and turn to Him for forgiveness.

PPP: David Repents.

WS 15 David Repents

Flipcharts Solomon

Note: When David died Solomon became king. After Solomon's death the kingdom split in half. The northern part was known as Israel and the southern part Judah. See worksheet and map on **'Divided Kingdom'** pages ....

WS 16 Final Plenary: Revelation & Faith – This is what I understand. This worksheet is very important because it will help pupils to see how the different parts of the module come together to show how God gradually reveals His plan for us.

The Kingdom Divided

> **Task:**
> Here is an outline of what happened when the kingdom was divided.
> Choose an 'eye catching' way, such as a tree map or mind map, to summarize the events to help you remember them.

The Kingdom divided

When King Solomon died the kingdom was divided, the northern part became known as *Israel* with Samaria its capital, and the southern part was *Judah* with Jerusalem as its capital city. Both Israel and Judah were ruled by kings, some were good, just rulers and followed God's law. Others ignored God and sought to gain riches and power.

Invasion and exile

Under the unjust rule of wicked kings the people began to worship other gods. God sent *prophets* like *Elijah* to warn his people that they were heading for disaster. Eventually both kingdoms were invaded. The *Assyrians* overran Israel and later the *Babylonians* conquered Judah. Solomon's great temple in Jerusalem was destroyed and the people were killed or carried off into *exile*.

The People of God in exile

The People of God felt lost and abandoned in Babylon. Their lives were difficult and they felt this was their punishment for forgetting God's laws.
They began to write about their sorrow. (These *psalms* are known as the *lamentations*). They also wrote down the stories we read in the Bible which had previously been passed by word of mouth. This helped to bring the people together and give them a sense of identity.

Hope in dark times

Since there was no temple where the people could worship they began to gather in synagogues. Synagogues gave them a place to pray, worship and read the scriptures. Stories of *Tobit* and *Esther* were important because they reminded people that even in exile it was possible to be faithful to God's law. The *prophets Isaiah* and *Ezekiel* promised the people that God would restore them to their homeland and bring them peace.

Some people return

After the people had been in exile for fifty years, the armies of the *Persian Empire* conquered Babylon. The Jews were allowed to return to their own country. Some chose to stay in the land of their exile as they had grown used to life there. The Jews who returned to Judah were allowed to rebuild the temple. They were guided by religious leaders like *Ezra* and *Nehemiah*.

An uncertain future

Although they were back in their own land, life was not easy for the People of God. They were overwhelmed by a succession of invading empires and often faced harsh *persecution*. About 160 BC *Judas Maccabeus* led a revolt and for a few years the *Jews* were *independent* of overlords. But gradually the People of God were coming to realise that God's promise of peace and kingdom had a deeper meaning. The idea of *salvation* and *life after death* began to evolve during this time.

Life under Roman rule

In 63 BC the Romans occupied the land and renamed it *Palestine*. They allowed the Jews to run their own religious council, the *Sanhedrin*. The Romans installed a cruel and ruthless man as king, *Herod the Great*. He was half-Jewish, but his actions were controlled by the Roman Governor. The people did not trust Herod but he tried to win popularity by building a magnificent *Second Temple*. The Romans were generally hated but a certain group of rich and privileged Jews, the priestly *Sadducees*, tried to accept them. On the other hand, the *Pharisees*, who prided themselves on following all religious laws and customs, tried to distance themselves from everything Roman.

Hopes for the Messiah change and grow

The People of God were still waiting for the fulfilment of God's promise of the Kingdom but now they began to have different ideas about how it would happen. A strict group, the *Essenes*, believed the Kingdom would be *heavenly*. The *Zealots*, who were religious freedom fighters, were sure it would be an *earthly* kingdom. *John the Baptist* began a movement which called for people to change their lives and *repent* of their sins to prepare for the coming of the Messiah.

The Story of God's People: from Abraham to Solomon

1800 BC

Abraham   Isaac   Jacob   Joseph

God makes a covenant with Abraham promising to make his descendants into a great nation. God asks Abraham to sacrifice his son, Isaac.

Isaac gives his blessing to his younger son, Jacob, instead. God's covenantal promise continues through Jacob and his descendants. Jacob 'wrestles' with God and receives the name 'Israel'. Jacob's son, Joseph, is sold as a slave by his brothers but eventually becomes the Pharaoh's overseer in Egypt. Jacob moves to Egypt to escape famine. He comes along with his 11 remaining sons and their families – the people of Israel. They increase in number and eventually become slaves of the Egyptians.

400 years in Egypt

Moses

Joshua

1200 BC

God asks Moses to help free the Israelites from Egyptian Slavery.

The People of Israel escape from Egypt by crossing the Red Sea. God makes a Covenant with the People of Israel on Mount Sinai. The People of Israel journey for 40 years through the wilderness to the land God promised them. Moses dies and Joshua leads Israel into the new land. His army captures the important city of Jericho.

The twelve tribes of Israel settle in the Promised Land and are led and protected by a succession of strong leaders, called Judges. God's prophet Samuel anoints Saul as the first King to rule over the twelve tribes. The Shepherd boy David defeats the Philistine warrior, Goliath. Saul loses God's favour and David becomes king. David establishes a secure kingdom by defeating neighbouring armies like the Philistines. David's son, Solomon, becomes King. He expands the kingdom, makes it rich and prosperous, and builds a magnificent temple for God.

200 years of Judges

900 BC

Kings

Saul

David

Solomon

1. Revelation and Faith **27**

2. God's Promises Fulfilled

Religious Education Curriculum Directory

"The action of God in the unfolding history of this covenant relationship and the variety of human response is revealed in the Scriptures of the Old and New Testament."

"God's Self-Revelation and the covenant relationship reach their fullness in Jesus Christ, the only-begotten Son of God" (page 14).

Key Learning Objectives:

Attainment Targets 1: Learning *about* the Catholic faith.
Attainment Targets 2: Learning *from* the Catholic faith.

- Understand the reasons for the exile of the Chosen People.
  o Identify similar aspects in the lives of people today.

- Reflect on the return from exile and God's plan for the Chosen People.
  o Think about what it means for us.

- Know how the birth of John the Baptist was foretold.
  o Reflect on what we can learn from it.

- Deepen our understanding of the Annunciation and Visitation.
  o Reflect on what we can learn from them.

- Know and reflect on the prophecy of Zechariah.
  o Consider the message it has for us today.

- Deepen our understanding of the birth of Jesus and the visit of the shepherds and wise men.
  o Think about how these events have shaped our lives.

2 Theological Notes

2 God Fulfils His Promises

Already, in the case of Abraham, God had promised to make of him "the father of a multitude of nations". Yet it is apparent that, in the course of history, God seemed to be allowing events to upset, and even frustrate, his own plan and design. Indeed, it makes God appear to be unfaithful to his own promises, for example, the near sacrifice of Isaac. God always surprises us with his "writing straight on what seem to be entirely crooked lines". God is the *God of surprises*. Is it strange, then, that the Bible always celebrates one singularly outstanding and never-failing quality of God's love and manner of loving - *God's faithfulness?* **God is faithful to his promises.**

Whether it is with regard to individual persons or groups and communities of persons, God's faithful love is highlighted over and over again in God's holy Word. This is particularly true of the "covenants" God made with human beings in the course of what we call the history of salvation – namely, God's gradual and pedagogical carrying out, in human history, of his plan and design of salvation.

We intend here, in these theological notes, to merely exemplify this consistent and unfailing faithfulness of God in fulfilling his promises by means, first, of the way he dealt with his chosen people, the people of Israel [A]; and, then, through the gospels of Matthew (Mt.) and Luke (Lk.) [B], with a particular accent placed on their very differently conceived *"infancy gospels"*, which distinctively focus on the person and mission of Jesus Christ, in whom God finally and definitively fulfils all his promises.

But, before we undertake all this, we need to focus, in this precise context of God's fulfilling his promises, on a very crucial theological and spiritual issue: that of *God's justice* in "punishing" those who **freely** choose to turn their backs on God and close their hearts to him, his life and his love.

I must admit that I often meet, in the carrying out of my ministry of the Spirit, with the following challenge hurled at me: "You are always speaking of God's love, Fr. Herbie; you never speak of God's justice! Why do you not balance off God's love with God's justice, seeing that the Bible itself so clearly, time and again, mentions God's justice?!"

Well, what is God's justice, in Christian terms? Principally in his letters to the Romans and the Galatians, St. Paul defines God's justice, in gospel terms, as that justice which makes us just. The word he uses in Greek for "justice" *(dikaiosyne)* is often translated as "righteousness", that righteousness of God which makes us righteous. This "justice" or "righteousness" of God, then, is no different from God's love, indeed, God's reconciling love which reaches out to us and renders us "just" or "righteous". The best way, perhaps, I can spell this out is to start with God's love – God, who is love. Now, because God loves us and, in his great love for us, has made us "free", he wants us freely and with open hearts to receive his love and gifts of love which he gives to, and showers on, us. He will never impose himself on us. We know from our own personal experience how we resist those who impose themselves on us; we fail to understand how such people protest that they "love" us. Of course, we do understand and willingly accept those who invite or attract or even solicit our freedom to do something or to avoid something else. This we readily understand and interpret as true love, because it respects our freedom. In this sense, God does, and frequently so, invite or attract or solicit our wills to what he knows is for our real good, real joy and real happiness; but he will never impose himself on us in this regard. He has in love gifted us with freedom, and he will in love respect this freedom of ours to the hilt.

Should I choose to say to God, "I do not want your love, you can keep it to yourself", God will fully respect my choice. *This kind of love* that God has for me is, in the last analysis, *God's justice:* that is, it is not God doing me any harm or punishing me, but I myself who do this, because I choose to close my heart to God. I have no one to blame for this except myself, in my closing self upon self.

It may help here, in this context, if I shared my own theological-spiritual understanding of what "hell" really is. My definition or description of "hell" can be couched thus: "I do not want to love, I do not want to be loved; just leave me to myself". If I am finally hardened in this life-attitude, precisely <u>this</u> is "<u>hell</u>" – not a place, but a state of my heart, closed in like a "cocoon" on myself and my freedom. In "hell", in this sense, there is <u>no</u> company; there cannot be. I am just with myself for ever – nothing more horrible than "I, with just me alone, for ever"!

[A] The Old Testament: the Chosen People

(a) Moses: The first and obvious way we can learn of God's ever faithful love towards the people he chose in love to be his own "chosen people" is to listen to Moses himself, whom God deputed to lead them from "slavery" to "freedom", from being "no people" to being "<u>his</u> chosen people". In the Book of Deuteronomy, Moses recounts this chosen people's ongoing history of being loved, and pursued in love, by God even when they repeatedly and stubbornly hardened their hearts to reject God and his covenants of love: "You are a people holy to the Lord, your God; the Lord, your God, has chosen you to be a people of his own possession, out of all the peoples that are on the face of the earth. It was not because you were more in number than any other people that the Lord set his love upon you and chose you, for you were the fewest of all people; but it is because the Lord loves you, and is keeping the oath which he swore to your fathers, that the Lord has brought you out with a mighty hand, and redeemed you from the house of bondage ... Know therefore that the Lord your God is God, the faithful God who keeps covenant and steadfast love ... to a thousand generations" (Deut. 7:6-9).

In forthright language, Moses continues: "Know, therefore, that the Lord is not giving you this land to possess because of your righteousness; for you are a stubborn people. ... Furthermore the Lord said to me, 'I have seen this people, and behold it is a stubborn people; let me alone, that I may destroy them and blot out their name from under heaven. ... So I lay prostrate before the Lord for these forty days and forty nights, because the Lord had said that he would destroy you. And I prayed to the Lord, 'O Lord God, destroy not your people and your heritage. ... Remember your servants Abraham, Isaac and Jacob; do not regard the stubbornness of this people or their wickedness or their sin. ... For they are your people and your heritage, whom you did bring out by your great power and your outstretched arm'" (Deut. 9:6, 13-14, 25-27, 29).

Right up to the conclusion of his mission, Moses would remind the whole assembly and people of Israel of God's relentless faithfulness in keeping and fulfilling his promises even in the face of their stubborn and stiff-necked resistance of infidelity to his covenant of love. So rang out the accents of his song in the ears of the entire assembly of Israel: "Give ear, O heavens, and I will speak ... For I will proclaim the name of the Lord, ascribe greatness to our God: a God of faithfulness and without iniquity, just and right is he. They have dealt corruptly with him, they are no longer his children because of their blemish; they are a perverse and wicked generation ... For the Lord's portion is his people, Jacob his allotted heritage.

He found him in a desert land ... he encircled him, he cared for him, he kept him as the apple of his eye. Like an eagle ... that flutters over its young, spreading out its wings, catching them, bearing them on its pinions, the Lord alone did lead him" (Deut. 32:1, 3-5, 9-12).

(b) Hosea: After Moses, we shall be helped to deepen our awareness of, and faith in, God's faithfulness in fulfilling his promises of love by taking up briefly the Book of the prophet Hosea, who ministers to the northern kingdom of Israel (also called "Ephraim" after its largest tribe). Outwardly, the nation is enjoying a time of prosperity and growth; but inwardly, moral corruption and spiritual adultery permeate the lives of the people. Hosea, instructed by God to marry a woman named Gomer, finds his domestic life to be an accurate and tragic dramatisation of the unfaithfulness of God's people. During his nearly fifty years of prophetic ministry, Hosea repeatedly returns, in God's name, to his threefold message: God abhors the sins of his people; judgement is certain; but God's loyal and faithful love remains and stands equally certain and firm forever. Hosea, whose name means "Salvation", offers, as God's messenger, the possibility of salvation to this people if only they would turn from idolatry back to God.

The *key* and central *message* of Hosea is *the faithful, loyal love of God for his people, Israel:* in fact, the themes of his prophecy's first three chapters echo throughout the rest of the book. The adultery of Gomer (chapter 1) illustrates the sin of Israel (chapters 4-7); the degradation of Gomer (chapter 2) represents the judgement of Israel (chapters 8-10); and Hosea's redemption of Gomer (chapter 3) pictures the restoration of Israel (chapters 11-14). In his relationship to Gomer, Hosea portrays God's unfailing faithfulness, justice, love and forgiveness towards his people.

It is in Hosea's prophecy that God's love for Israel takes on profoundly delicate, even maternally tender, accents of affection, and this, in the face of repeated rejection: "When Israel was a child, I loved him, and out of Egypt I called my son. The more I called them, the more they went away from me; they kept sacrificing to the Baals and burning incense to idols. Yet it was I who taught Ephraim to walk. I took them up in my arms; but they did not know that I healed them. I led them with cords of compassion, with the bands of love, and I became to them as one who eases the yoke on their jaws, and I stooped down to them and fed them" (Hos. 11:1-4).

Do we human beings not tend to judge our God the way we judge one another, with our human norms and standards? God is God – God, who is love, and not one to be judged and appraised by our human standards and worldly norms. Precisely in the very context in which we were listening to Hosea's statement of God's tender love for his recalcitrant people, we hear these remarkable words of God: "My people are bent on turning away from me ... How can I give you up, O Ephraim! How can I hand you over, O Israel! ... My heart recoils within me, my compassion grows warm and tender. I will not execute my fierce anger, I will not again destroy Ephraim; for **I am God and not man**, the Holy One in your midst, and I will not come to destroy" (Hos. 11: 7-9). Such words touch us deeply, for God appears to be well nigh pleading with us: "Do not judge me as you judge one another. Remember always, **"I am God, and not man!"**

(c) Isaiah and Jeremiah: Yet, with all this, it is the later great prophets Isaiah and Jeremiah who powerfully communicate to us, in the continuing, chequered history of the chosen people, God's never-failing faithfulness in keeping the Covenant and fulfilling his promises of saving and redeeming them in love.

<u>Isaiah's</u> prophetic ministry, spanning the reigns of four kings of Judah, covers at least forty years. His prophecy has been called "the entire Bible in miniature". Indeed, the first thirty-nine chapters are filled with judgement on immoral and idolatrous men and women. Judah has sinned; the surrounding nations have sinned; the whole earth has sinned. God cannot allow that such blatant sin go unpunished for ever. And yet, the final twenty-seven chapters declare an unambiguous, unmistakable message of hope: the Messiah is coming as a Saviour and a conquering King who will, yes, bear a Cross, but precisely so, will wear a triumphant crown of glory. The prophet's name "Isaiah" *(Yesha 'yahu)* means "Yahweh is Salvation", so that his very name becomes an excellent summary of the entire Book named after him.

As Isaiah's name suggests, Salvation comes from God, not from men or human resources. God is clearly proclaimed as the supreme Ruler, the sovereign Lord of history and the only Saviour. Because the nation (Judah) does not turn away from its sinful practices, Isaiah announces the ultimate overthrow of Judah. Nevertheless, God remains, and will remain, faithful to his covenant by preserving a godly remnant; God promises salvation and liberation through the coming Messiah. The Saviour will come out of Judah, and accomplish the dual work of redemption and restoration. The Gentiles will come to his light and, with God making all things anew, a universal blessing will finally take place.

The **Book of Jeremiah** is the prophecy of a man divinely called in his youth – in effect, when still a teenager. He comes across as a heartbroken prophet with a heartbreaking message, who labours for more than forty years preaching a message of doom to the stiff-necked people of Judah. Despised and persecuted by his countrymen, Jeremiah bathes his harsh prophecies in tears of compassion. Even though revealing himself as heartbroken, he forthrightly declares, through his sermons and signs, God's unstinting faithfulness in keeping his promises in love, even to the point of establishing a "new covenant".

Jeremiah's name literally means, "Yahweh throws", perhaps in the sense of laying a foundation; it could effectively be equivalent to: "Yahweh establishes, appoints or sends". In Jeremiah, God is shown to be patient and holy: he delays judgement and appeals to his people to repent before it is too late. As the object lesson at the potter's house demonstrates, a ruined vessel can be repaired while still wet (Jer. 18:1-4); but, once dried, a marred vessel is fit only for the garbage heap (Jer. 19:10-11). God's warning is clear: Judah's time for repentance will soon pass. Because the people defy God's words and refuse to repent, the Babylonian captivity and exile are inevitable. While Jeremiah courageously and forthrightly foretells, in God's name, the people's coming catastrophe, he also unambiguously proclaims God's gracious and faithful promise of hope and restoration. There will surely be a good and holy remnant of God's people; indeed, God will establish a "new covenant" (Jer. 31:31-34). It is the Messiah who will institute this covenant by means of his death and resurrection – his paschal passage.

[B] The New Testament: the Gospels of Matthew (Mt.) and of Luke (Lk.)

The **Gospel of Matthew (Mt.)** is the gospel written by a Jew to Jews about a Jew; in other words, it is a Jewish tax-collector named Matthew (called Levi, before he decided to leave all and follow Jesus), writing to clearly Jewish readers to convince them that their "expected King of the Jews" has come: Jesus Christ is the "King of the Jews", the long-awaited Messiah. Through a carefully selected series of Old Testament quotations, Matthew documents Jesus Christ's claim to be the Messiah. His genealogy, his miraculous birth and obscure – yet carefully prophesied – birthplace, his flight into Egypt, his announcement by John the Baptist, his baptism, his battle with Satan in the wilderness, his messages and miracles all point to, and support, the same inescapable conclusion: Jesus is the culmination-fulfilment of God's promises delivered by the prophets over a period of a thousand years. God's redemptive plan and design are alive and well, even after four hundred years of prophetic silence – the last of the prophets (Haggai, Zechariah, Malachi), who prophesied after the exile to the remnant of God's people, had already died four hundred years before Jesus Christ.

The **Gospel of Luke (Lk.)** is the gospel of "the Son of Man". Luke, a physician, writes with the compassion and human warmth of a family doctor, as he carefully documents the integral and captivating humanity of the Son of Man, who is also truly Son of God – Jesus Christ. Luke emphasises Jesus' ancestry, tracing it back to the first man, Adam; he details Jesus' birth, and traces Jesus' early years up to the age of twelve, before moving carefully through his earthly ministry, which commences after his baptism and temptations in the desert. Luke, who was himself very probably of non-Jewish, gentile origin, had a clear and pointed aim in his gospel account, namely, to strengthen the faith of non-Jewish, gentile believers and stimulate faith among non-believers. In doing this, he highlights the fact that Christ was not only divine, but fully human, portraying Christ in his fullest humanity by emphasising, more than any other gospel, Christ's human warmth and feelings. What stands out in the message of Luke is that God, through Jesus Christ, "has come to seek and save that which was lost" (Lk. 19:10) – a Jesus with a heart that identifies with the sorrow and plight of sinful men and women, in order to help them bear their sorrows and afflictions, so that, through them, they may receive the gift of love he offers them from God: salvation.

Matthew's infancy gospel (Mt.1-2) is, in keeping with his own clear aim of a Jew writing for Jews, meant to portray Jesus as the "new Israel" persecuted from early on in his infancy, then fleeing into exile and from that exile, by divine intervention, returning to the "promised land". Very differently, Luke's infancy gospel (Lk. 1-2) presents, in a particularly new light, the infant Jesus, after the events preceding his birth which include the birth announcement of Jesus' herald and forerunner, John the Baptist and his own, then the Baptist's birth and his own birth. What is this particularly new light shed by Luke on the infant Jesus? Luke presents this infant as *__on the road to Jerusalem__* from his earliest years: at the time of his circumcision and, then, his presentation in the Temple (Lk. 2:21-30); and again, when he is twelve years old and goes to celebrate the Passover with Mary and Joseph, up to the Temple where he is lost and found (Lk. 2:39-50). This, in Luke's intent, is a principal theological theme that runs through this gospel, reaching its explicit climax from the time that Jesus "steadfastly set his face to go up to Jerusalem" [Lk. 9:51; indeed, all of the dramatic peak of Jesus' public ministry (Lk. 9:51 -19:27) reaching up to the grand finale of his passion, death and resurrection (Lk.19:28 – 24:53)]. What this main theological theme of Luke is symbolically focusing on is Jesus' passage from this unredeemed world to the Father, from "slavery" to "freedom", from "death" to "life": his paschal passage or mystery.

In Luke, then, Jesus' public ministry following on from his baptism and temptations (Lk 3:21-22; 4:1-13) is inaugurated with his programmatic messianic announcement in the synagogue of Nazareth, based on Is. 61:1-2 (Lk 4:16-30); this messianic message is lived out thereafter, step by step, right up to its climax. Already at Jesus' presentation in the Temple, the holy old man Simeon, filled with the Holy Spirit, had prophesied: "Behold, this child is set for the fall and rising of many in Israel, for a sign of contradiction" (Lk 2:34). In such a mounting crescendo surrounding the person and ministry of Jesus, growing belief and growing opposition develop side by side: those who believe are challenged by the cost of discipleship, whereas those who oppose will not be satisfied until the Son of man hangs lifeless on a cross. But Christ's resurrection ensures that God's promises and God's plan of "seeking out and saving that which was lost" are completely fulfilled and victoriously vindicated.

Herbert Alphonso SJ

Additional Suggestions and Resources

Understand the reasons for the exile of the Chosen People. Identify similar aspects in the lives of people today.

[Note: In the Assessment Folder on the DVD for this module there are approximately fourteen assessment tasks and four assessment sheets mapped to the Bishops' Conference Levels of Attainment in Religious Education.]

Starting point:
Help pupils to empathise with refugees, asylum seekers and situations where people are driven from their homeland. Make links with current situations in the world and take time to thank God for the peace and the comforts that we have. Explain how easy it is to become complacent and take everything for granted.

Make links and prepare for classroom discussion:
Many people in different parts of the world are uprooted from their homeland and become exiles because of conflict. Teacher provides examples.

Work in groups: choose a country to research.
   a) Why are people leaving the country?

b) Who is responsible for it?

c) Are all the population suffering?

d) Who suffers most?

e) How do they suffer?

f) What do they need most of all?

g) What do others do to help?

Use IWB to draw together the common causes.

- Ask pupils if they think there are people who live in exile in this country?
- Who are they?
- Do they know of anyone who had to leave his or her country?
- Did they receive a welcome and help?
- What it was like for them?

WS 1 Ruvimbo's experience.

(Note: Ruvimbo is from Zimbabwe and her name means HOPE. Dai Jones, her teacher at Villiers High School in Ealing, said that refugee students feel that stereotypical images of refugees cause them huge problems and even distract people from the real issues. It will help if you explain to students the difference between political refugees, with well educated parents who enjoyed tremendous influence and esteem in their original homelands, and those who are migrants or victims of horrendous natural events and wars.)

Flipchart: Key words and starter [Exile (1)].

Explain that we are going to study the reasons for the exile of the Chosen People. Invite pupils to use bullet points to list the reasons in the order they think are the most serious. Then, make links with our experience today.

Other Resource on DVD:

- Overview of Divided Kingdom.

PPP Reasons for Exile

WS 2 - Pupil's Book page 25 Worksheet 'Exile of Jews'

PPP Exile: Longing for God – the faithful Jews never gave up hope and their yearning for God is expressed in Psalm 41 (42) 'Like the deer that yearns for running streams ....'

Rabbi Hugo Gryn in Auschwitz

Reflect on how religious faith is tested by bad experiences:. Rabbi Hugo Gryn, who had survived the concentration camp at Auschwitz, shared something of his experience. He said that as he was driven into this dreadful camp he saw hundred of Jewish phylacteries at the entrance. The phylacteries are very small black leather boxes which contain four sacred readings from the Bible in Hebrew; devout Jews wear them on their arms or even on their foreheads during morning prayers on days other than the Sabbath. They are a sign of devotion and of commitment to the Law. Yet these same devout Jews had thrown them away out of despair as they were driven into the concentration camp. They had lost their faith and felt that God was letting them down.

Hopefully, we will never be faced with something as awful as being sentenced to a concentration camp but we might think of some things that might happen that could cause us to doubt our faith.

Discuss times when FAITH is tested.
a) What are some of the things that could happen to cause us to doubt our faith?
b) What can we do now to help us to remain faithful to God when trouble comes?
c) What examples can we recall of other people who trusted in God in difficult times? *[Opportunity to re-cap on Abraham].*

Website to explain Temple: The Temple Institute: Mikdash Kids Home Page
www.templeinstitute.org
www.templeinstitute.org/kids/mikdash_kids.htm

> ## Know about the return from Exile and God's plan for the Chosen People. Think about what they mean for us.

Starting point:
Think about what happens when disaster strikes. For example, the town or village is flooded; there is a very bad storm and there is no electricity. What effect does it have on people? Some will be very generous and go out to help others who are worse off, particularly very elderly people and families with small children. Disaster often brings many unforeseen blessings.

Take time to reflect on what the Jews understood during the exile and how they benefited from the experience. Invite pupils to make a **'Remember'** note for
themselves based on what they can learn from the experience of the Jewish people.

Flipcharts: Starter with pictures of floods and activity 1 [Exile (2).]

Activities
1. God has built ***healing*** into our bodies and into our lives if we trust him.
a) Think of situations where 'time is a great healer', for example,

- Freak floods – waiting for the water to go down;
- A physical wound – takes time to heal;
- A virus – needs to run its course

b) Think of situations where God renews our strength

2. Pupils learn the meaning of the Key Words in this section. They could use the new words to make sentences to show the meaning.

Prophecies: Remind pupils that the prophecies were made approximately five hundred years before the birth of Jesus. Jesus is the fulfilment of these prophecies. His power is at work in the lives of people today who recognise their need for God and completely trust in him.

'Exile Freedom to Return' [Assessment Folder worksheet for assessment].

Make links between the Old and New Testaments: Without the OT we would not fully understand the NT. The NT is the fulfilment of the OT. God's face was veiled and hidden in the OT. In the NT it is fully and perfectly revealed in Jesus. In the scripture, we find trustworthy and reliable testimony, a first hand account of those who saw Him with their eyes, heard Him with their ears and touched Him with their own hands *(The Gift of Scripture, 44)*.

Activities
WS 3 Bridge Map OT to NT.

PPP 'Suffering Servant Prophecies fulfilled in NT'.

'Suffering Servant Prophecies' [Assessment Folder: use for more able pupils].

> ## Deepen our understanding of the Annunciation and Visitation.
> ## Reflect on what we can learn from them.

Starting point: Discuss what we understand by faith? What examples have we studied of people of great faith? Make links with Abraham, Sarah. Can anyone suggest why Mary is seen as the 'model of faith'?

Reflect:
- Does God just speak to anybody? *(Those seeking and searching for Him)*.
- Remember the Jewish people during the exile. Who did God save? *(Those who never gave up hope, but bowed low before God in total surrender to His will)*.
- Why do you think He saved them? *(God's power is greatest when people are aware of their own inadequacy)*.

Mary was humble, poor, unknown and her heart was open and ready to do God's will. So, when God spoke to Mary through the Angel Gabriel, her response was not "I'll do it", but "Let what you have said be done to me." We call Mary's 'Yes' to God the Marian 'fiat' (from the Latin facere = to do, to make).

Mary knew that she could not do it but she was ready and willing to let God work through her. She understood that it was only through the power of God that she could become the mother of God's Son.

How can we be like Mary? The best way is to make time each day to pray and ask Jesus to be with us. Ask him for the grace to seek him. Pray that we may see him more clearly, love him and be willing to follow him. **Pause for silent personal prayer.**

Other Resources Folder:
Circle Time: Reflection on Mary. Teacher needs to cut up the questions.

Flipcharts: Reflection on Mary – content is the same as for Circle Time; to be used as an alternative to it.

2. **WS 4 'Mary's Song of Praise'** for less able pupils.

3. Through Mary's words and life, God could revolutionise the way we **THINK, ACT** and **LIVE**.
   a) Think about the importance we attach to money, power, status, brains, and good looks.
   b) In pairs, work out how God could change your life.
   c) How might this affect the way you live and treat others?

4. Work in pairs:
It is said that in Mary's Magnificat there are three revolutions:
   a) an 'economic' revolution;
   b) a 'political' revolution;
   c) a 'moral' revolution;
   • Look up the meaning of economic, political and moral.
   • Pupils divide into three parties: (i) economic, (ii) political, (iii) moral and subdivide again (if you wish) to work in smaller groups.
   • Each pupil reads the Magnificat in silence and writes down the phrases that apply to his/her party.
   • Each group tries to work out the revolution that could or has taken place for people who hand their lives over to God.
   • Then they prepare to make a presentation of their finding to the class.

WS 5 'Mary's Magnificat'.
'Mary's Prophecy' [Assessment folder for worksheet]

Meaning and example of Revolution:

Revolution means a 'total change'. Take the example of computers; they have revolutionised the way we work. We can now switch on by pushing a button and we have thousands of pieces of information available to us. Within seconds we can send a document to any part of the world. We no longer have to keep information in our head – it can all go on the computer.

Flipcharts: Reflection on Mary & Joseph.

> ### Know and reflect on the prophecy of Zechariah.
> ### Consider the message it has for us today.

Starting points for reflection:

In Elizabeth's day, it was considered a humiliation if a married woman did not have children. She was to be pitied by some and talked about by others. Elizabeth waited, dreaming, hoping and trusting in God. As we have seen in the life of Abraham's wife, Sarah, God's ways are mysterious: prayers are answered but not in the way and time expected.

Like Sarah, it was only when Elizabeth was old and well past childbearing age that God intervened. Her cousin, Mary, came to hear her good news and to share her own. They recognised each other as being filled with God's grace. Their unborn children joined in: "Now as soon as Elizabeth heard Mary's greeting, the child leapt in her womb and Elizabeth was filled with the Holy Spirit. She gave a loud cry and said, 'Of all women you are the most blessed, and blessed is the fruit of your womb. Why should I be honoured with a visit from the mother of my Lord? For the moment your greeting reached my ears, the child in my womb leapt for joy'" (Lk. 41-44).

It was Elizabeth who declared that the baby's name would be John. She dismissed the protests of relatives and friends who wanted to follow the custom of naming the baby after his father. Elizabeth heard the voice of God in silence – his name shall be John!

Key points to help understand Zechariah's prophecy:

- God has kept His covenantal promise.
- The Saviour is coming to save us from our sins, to redeem us.
- His only son, John, is going to be God's prophet.
- John will prepare the way for Jesus when he comes.
- John will let the people know that they will have salvation, that is, fullness of life now and hereafter, because all their sins will be forgiven.
- All this will happen through the loving kindness and mercy of God who is coming to us in Jesus.

Flipcharts: Zechariah.

Worksheet in Teacher's Book page 42 Zechariah's Prophecy: the Benedictus – pupils work in pairs on a sentence to explain its meaning.

PPP Zechariah.

Action Plan: the message for us is: **LET GO, LET GOD.**
Try to give God a real and serious chance to be God in your life.
Allow Him to speak to you. In order for that to happen make a plan to choose a quiet place to be alone with God for 5-10 minutes. Begin by reading a few lines from Luke 1 and then let go and be with God who is with you.

Prayer:

Lord Jesus, grant that we may be open to your Spirit at work in our lives each day. Help us to make time for you and to be able recognise your presence in our hearts. Come, Lord Jesus come and make your home with us.

Background:

Zechariah and Elizabeth lived in a village in the hill country of Judaea, along the ridge of coastland close to the mountains south of Jerusalem. Around this area the hill country was a wilderness, even described as an uninhabited desert. This is where John grew up staying close to God because he was to be the one to prepare the nation for the Messiah.

Deepen our understanding of the birth of Jesus and visit of shepherds and wise men.
Think about how these events have shaped our lives.

Starting point:

Take time to reflect on the reasons why God came to earth. What does it all mean for us? (There is an additional theological paper on 'Original Sin' on page 84 for the teacher).

PPP 'Moses' – This PPP is here in case there is a need to recapitulate on the part Moses played in salvation history.

Pause to reflect: Answers for Pupil's Book page 37
Who Is This Baby?
- He is the 'SAVIOUR';
- He is the 'CHRIST';
- He is the 'LORD'.

Where Is He Born?
- Born in a stable;
- Laid in a manger;
- Wrapped in rags.

Audio recording **'Innkeeper's wife reflects on the first Christmas'.**

Who Welcomes Him?
- Lowly shepherds

Additional Resource on DVD: Map of Nativity.

Reactions to Jesus: Pupil's Book page 39
No sooner is Jesus born than people start reacting to him in very definite ways.
- SHEPHERDS spread the GOOD NEWS;
- KING HEROD was hostile and planned to destroy Jesus;
- WISE MEN – foreigners from the East, looking for the true God, worshipped HIM.

PPP 'God's Promises Fulfilled – Nativity'.

WS 6 Scripture & Art: Nativity using the Pupil's Book page 36.

WS 7 Important Plenary: 'God's promises fulfilled and how they relate to our lives today'.

Fulfilment of God's Plan [Assessment Folder for worksheet for assessment.]

WS 8 Christmas cards for less able pupils. *(Teacher will need a collection of religious Christmas cards for pupils to use).*

Additional Resource on DVD: Drama 'The Shepherds' for collective worship.

WS 9 Make a 'coat-hanger' poem about St. Joseph.

Background information:
Shepherds were despised by the orthodox who carefully observed the Law. The shepherds could not observe all the meticulous rules and regulations such as hand-washings, etc. They were looked down upon as very common people.

Magi: In those times, many people believed in astrology. They believed they could foretell the future from the stars and that their destiny was settled by the star under which they were born. We cannot tell which star they saw but it seemed to speak to them of the entry of a king into the world. Herod told the magi that he too wished to come to worship the child – but his desire was to murder the child born to be king.

Gifts: Gold is for a king. Frankincense is for a priest. Myrrh is the gift for one who is to die. Myrrh was used to embalm the bodies of the dead. It was foretold that the true king would be the perfect High Priest and Saviour who would die for us.

THE BENEDICTUS – Zechariah's Prophecy

Task:

Work in pairs. Take one sentence of the Benedictus and explain its meaning.

"Blessed be the Lord, the God of Israel!

He has visited his people and redeemed them.

He has raised up for us a mighty saviour

in the house of David his servant,

as he promised by the lips of holy men,

those who were his prophets from of old.

A saviour who would free us from our foes,

from the hands of all who hate us.

So his love for our fathers is fulfilled

and his holy covenant remembered.

He swore to Abraham our father to grant us,

that free from fear, and from the hands of our foes,

we might serve him in holiness and justice

all the days of our life in his presence.

As for you, little child,

you shall be called a prophet of God, the most High.

You shall go ahead of the Lord

to prepare his ways before him,

to make known to his people their salvation

through forgiveness of all their sins,

the loving-kindness of the heart of our God

who visits us like the dawn from on high.

He will give light to those in darkness,

those who dwell in the shadow of death,

and guide us into the way of peace (Lk. 1: 68-79).

God's Promises Fulfilled

What were God's promises?

What did the people have to learn?

How did the prophets help the people?

Who handed over their lives to God?

What happened to them?

Who did God choose to bring about His promise?

How did this person respond?

What can we learn from this?

What does the fulfilment of this promise mean for us today?

How is it going to help you?

Are all God's promises fulfilled? If not, what do you think needs to happen?

3. The Saviour

Religious Education Curriculum Directory

"Jesus is truly God and, as a man, truly human. His life, death and resurrection are the central event of all human history and at the heart of faith. His cross is a sign of his unique offering of himself for each and every human being. As truly God, Jesus reveals the truth and love of God; as truly human, Jesus reveals the perfect response to God and intimate communion with his Father – 'Abba'.

"As human persons we desire the good, yet human nature bears the wound of original sin and is subject to temptation. It is in Christ that the gift of eternal life is assured. It is in him that the perfection of human dignity is revealed. It is he who teaches the way of happiness" for example, in the Beatitudes." (Pages 14 & 34).

Key learning objectives:

Attainment Targets 1: Learning *about* the Catholic faith.
Attainment Targets 2: Learning *from* the Catholic faith.

- Deepen our awareness of the message of John the Baptist.
  o Reflect on the demands it makes on us.

- Know that Jesus came to show us that HE is the WAY to the Father.
  o Consider what this means for us.

- Understand that Jesus came to help all people come close to God.
  o Reflect on how Jesus works through Christians today.

- Understand that Jesus is the Messiah.
  o Reflect on what this means for us.

- Know that Jesus is truly God and, as man, truly human.
  o Reflect on what this means for us.

- Understand what Jesus asks of us.
  o Reflect on who Jesus is for us.

- Reflect on some people who lived for Jesus.
  o Think of what we can learn from them.

3 Theological Notes

3 The Saviour

[A] Background: "Salvation" and "The Saviour"

Divine Revelation, especially as mediated through the written Word of God, has captured in the term "salvation" one of the deepest and most essential aspects of the gracious, loving action of God for and among us human beings, in our history. In the Bible, both in the Old and New Testaments, salvation is a key term, even a central unifying theme. It is freely offered to *all* human beings (cf. 1 Tim. 2:4; 4:10), not just as individual persons, but as a "people" [cf. the central Exodus-event with texts such as Ex. 14:13; Is. 63:8ff; Ps. 106 (105): 8, 10, 21]. It is God, then, who has the primacy and takes the initiative in salvation. Salvation is directed not only to all human beings, but in each one to the whole human person, matter and spirit. It is then to reach not only human beings but, through them, the entire cosmos itself. If human beings – and, through them, the cosmos itself – are to be saved, the obvious implication is that all human beings, both each single person and the whole human race as such, indeed the whole sweep of creation, (cf. Rom. 8:21-23) are in a situation which stands in need of "salvation" – some sort of "danger" or "peril" from which they need to be rescued or, shall we say, some sort of "bondage" or "slavery" from which they need to be freed and liberated.

At its root, this "danger"/"peril", "bondage"/ "slavery" is that of sin – personal sin which then, gathering momentum in the heart of human persons, gradually becomes crystallised in, and as it were built up into, what we are today calling societal structures of sin. Sin, we all know, can in its inmost theological essence be best summed up in the following terms: the free creature, becoming so conscious of and fascinated with its freedom, that it raises this freedom to the plane of "the absolute", thus closing itself upon itself, and in the end finds only itself. In the last analysis, then, sin is concentrated selfishness – individual selfishness, widened then to societal and structured selfishness.

It is radically this reality of sin-selfishness that is touched by the saving action of God. What is noteworthy from the start is that God works out in action his plan of salvation *patiently and pedagogically* in the course of *real history, a history of salvation*: in effect, a long drawn-out and patient *prefiguring and preparation*, **first**, in the history of the people of the Old Covenant (Israel) leading to the coming of Jesus Christ, God's Messiah and Saviour; **then**, the unfolding of the *actual effecting* of the work of salvation in the Saviour's infancy, life, passion, death, resurrection and ascension (his *paschal mystery*); **still further**, beginning with the stupendous outpouring of God's Holy Spirit in the Pentecost event, *the ongoing continuation and application*, in the power of the Spirit, *of God's saving work* already accomplished in Jesus Christ *through the mediation of the Church* and its mission/ministry of word and sacrament – the Church which is the People of the New Covenant assembled and constituted in and through the aforementioned paschal mystery of the Saviour Jesus Christ; **finally**, all of this history culminating in the glorious realisation and eschatological (final; at the end of time) consummation of God's plan of salvation with the Second Coming of the Lord, with "his handing over the Kingdom to God the Father, having done away with every sovereignty, authority and power … so that God may be all in all" (1 Cor. 15:24-28).

Two elements stand out in bold relief in this "background overview" we have just traced: first, that *real daily life* and *real daily experience* lived out in *real history* as it gradually unfolds, are crucial factors chosen by God himself in his working out of salvation *patiently, pedagogically, historically*; secondly, that this God-initiated and God-given salvation is not, in the first instance, a wondrously well-knit organic body of truths or doctrine which must be faithfully adhered to, nor even, primarily, an admirable code of ethical and moral conduct to be conscientiously observed; it is, at its core and above all, a *Person, the Saviour Jesus Christ*. He is *himself* the "salvation" offered and gifted by God; his *personal* mystery is the mystery of salvation. "For God so loved the world that he gave his only Son, that whoever believes in him should not perish but have eternal life. For God sent the Son into the world ... that the world might be saved through him" (Jn. 3:16-17); and, as the First Letter of St. John roundly confirms: "And we have seen and testify that the Father has sent his Son as the Saviour of the world" (1 Jn. 4:14).

[B] The Saviour's Mystery

Is there one succinct and compact manner in which we can capture the entire mystery of Jesus Christ our "Saviour"? For this, I personally find great inspiration in St. John's Gospel, as he closes his account of Christ's crucifixion with his contemplation of the pierced side of Jesus: "One of the soldiers pierced his side with a spear, and at once there came out blood and water. He who saw it has borne witness – his testimony is true, and he knows that he tells the truth – so that you also may believe. For these things took place that the scripture might be fulfilled, 'Not a bone of his shall be broken'. And again another scripture says, 'They shall look on him whom they have pierced'" (Jn.19: 34-37).

In this testimony of John, we cannot help noting that he becomes extremely solemn, using such words as, "He who has seen it has borne witness – his testimony is true, and he knows that he tells the truth – so that you also may believe". Why this unexpected, almost outlandish, solemnity?! Is it something strange, we ask, that from a dead man's heart, pierced with a spear soon after his death, there should ooze out the last drops of blood and water (shall we say, 'serum liquid' or 'lymph')? But John is clearly not referring to 'blood' and 'water' in a purely physiological sense; he is evoking 'water' and 'blood' such as these were understood in a whole rich and consistent biblical tradition.

In this profound and consistent tradition, **'Water'** symbolises the life that God gives, very particularly in messianic times, so much so that, in such a period of accomplishment (the New Testament), it stands for the Spirit of God whom the Risen Jesus gives. To trace this briefly through the Bible, we have an example **in the Old Testament** in *Is. 12:3* ("you will draw water with joy from the springs of salvation") and **in the New Testament** in *Jn. 4:14* (Jesus to the Samaritan woman: "the water that I shall give will become in that person a spring of water welling up to eternal life". As for **'Blood': in the Old Testament**, it symbolises the many ritual sacrifices, in blood, of animals (bulls, goats, heifers) [cf. *Ex. 24:5-6,8; Heb. 9:7, 11-14, 19-22, 25-26, 28*]; **in the New Testament**, it stands for the blood of the Lamb of God poured out for the salvation of the world [cf. *Mt. 26:27-28; Mk. 14:23-24; Lk. 22:20-21; Heb. 10:4-7, 19-20*].

In a word, then, **'water'** stands for Jesus' giving himself totally or "handing himself over" out of love, in the name of his Father, to us men and women of all times and all places; and **'blood'** stands for Jesus' giving himself totally or "handing himself over", from our human side, to the Father, as **the** perfect sacrifice of obedience and expiation. Therefore, **both** Jesus' handing himself over in love from the Father's side to us, namely, the giving of his Spirit [= *WATER*]; **and** Jesus' handing himself over from our side of human beings to the Father: the pouring out of his *BLOOD* in obedience and expiation. Is not, then, "blood" and "water" a complete summing up of the entire mystery of Jesus as "mediator": from the Father to us men and women, and from us men and women to the Father? This, indeed, explains John's unexpected solemnity in his contemplation of the pierced side of the Saviour from which flowed "blood" and "water".

[C] The Saviour's Values, Standards and Criteria

If the Saviour's mystery can be succinctly summed up as the "handing himself over in love" to the Father and, in the Father, to us men and women of all times and places, then *what characterises and distinguishes the Saviour in his person and in his entire* mission is precisely such "**handing over of self in love**". Such a distinguishing trait or criterion may be spelt out as follows: **Jesus Christ gets out of himself and all forms of human selfishness to give and surrender himself in love to his Father and, in the Father, to us men and women – indeed, to all creation and the entire cosmos.**

Consequently, those who call themselves the Saviour's followers, Jesus Christ's disciples, namely, '**Christians**', will be genuinely and authentically such only if their persons, lives and activity carry the distinguishing mark or criterion that is the singular trait of their Lord and Master, Jesus Christ: **handing over of self in love**. In fact, Jesus himself formulated this in a very definitive sentence when he declared: "If anyone will come after me, let that person renounce self, take up his/her cross and follow me" (Mt. 16:24). This is not, as it may seem, the formulation of a triple criterion of being an authentic disciple of Jesus Christ. It is only the affirmation of three ways of *one single, unique* criterion of the "cost of discipleship". This *one single criterion* is the "*cross of Jesus Christ*" in its profound theological and spiritual sense. Do we Christians not assert spontaneously with a certain "Christian" instinct – and how right we are! – that if something does not bear the sign or seal of the "cross of Jesus", it is **not** 'Christian'? What, then, do we mean by the "cross of Jesus"? This "cross" is not necessarily physical – nor even moral – suffering, which certainly is one form of the "cross of Jesus". This "cross" is always and unfailingly "the handing over of self in love" – that is, the getting out of self to hand over self to God and, in God, to others – and all this, in love. No wonder, Jesus affirms so categorically what, for him, is the essence of the "cost of discipleship": to "renounce self", which is precisely what his "cross" stands for in love; this, then, is to "follow Jesus".

This is why the "cross of Jesus" denotes and connotes not just his "death", but also his "resurrection", for his **love**, while handing over himself, could not have been more **alive** than when Jesus died on the cross – his **love**, at this moment, is **at once death and resurrection**, one single mystery of handing over self in love. Such "handing over self in love, can be tersely termed *INNER FREEDOM*, which can be explicated thus: freedom **from** self and all forms of selfishness, in order to become free **for** God and, in God, free **for** others.

What, then, can we designate as the Saviour's distinctive values? In a nutshell, they could all very well and significantly be termed "inner freedom" or "spiritual freedom", which is a gift of the Holy Spirit of God – as St. Paul proclaims categorically: "Where the Spirit of the Lord is, there is freedom" (2 Cor. 3:17).

It would be worthwhile linking this up, somewhat in detail, with what we have earlier described as God's gift of "Salvation", carried out and accomplished finally in the person and mission of the unique Saviour, Jesus Christ. If salvation is God's freely-communicated gift, initiated by his love and concern to save human beings – and, through them, the whole cosmos – at root and basically from the bondage of sin-selfishness with its multi-pronged societal ramifications, then it devolves essentially on the human person freely and responsibly to actively receive this gift of God in the *real* human experience of daily living.

However, precisely that everyday experience teaches us that none of us is spontaneously free in the heart, or open, to the gift of God's saving love, blocked and impeded as we tend to be by our many likes and dislikes, our attachments and repugnance, our prejudices and inhibitions, enslaved, in the last analysis, by such spontaneous feelings and judgements degenerating into veritable attitudes of self-love, self-will and self-interest. Thus it is only the act of "faith", which theologically is, at its heart, the human person's free opening of self, or gift and surrender of self, to the self-giving God that is the real starting-point, on the human person's side, of the *experience of salvation*. For God, as biblical revelation so powerfully inculcates, never ceases to come to us with his saving love, be it through other persons or events or circumstances of time, place and action. It is not God who is short-handed; it is we, human beings, who are not ready or "free" – or, as some masters of the spiritual life love to say (notably St. Ignatius of Loyola), "disposed" – for God who is always coming into our lives.

And so, the ongoing adventure of the growing, maturing experience of salvation for us human beings is daily, progressively and pedagogically in our real history and experience – certainly, under the action of the ever-coming God (for the primacy and initiative belong to God) – to become more and more "free", that is, to actively allow God to *free us progressively from* all those barriers that block his salvific love and life and power, in order to become more and more *free for* God, more and more available to God's saving power and action in us, thus becoming, in him, more and more *free for* our brothers and sisters. In other words, in this way we become channels and instruments of God's saving presence and action for our brothers and sisters.

On our human side, therefore, the dynamic path of the maturing experience of salvation is really the experiential process of growth in "inner freedom" – in both dimensions of growing "freedom from" and of progressive "freedom for". This latter "freedom for", which is rightly termed "availability" or "active receptivity", really entails increasing openness to God's Holy Spirit and to his gifts. By these gifts the Spirit, who is the personal self-giving love of God, leads us. Through these gifts he urges us to those active purifications and accomplishes in us those passive purifications (be it noted, "purification" is another word for areas or zones of "liberation" or "freedom"), which are so necessary for profound union with God, that is the deepening experience of salvation.

There could be no more instructive way for us to grasp and then assimilate and live out, the Saviour's values in our daily lives than to reflect in our hearts on the **Beatitudes** (or 'Blessings') – *either* eight of them, such as Mt. 5:3-10 proposes them, *or* in the way St. Luke proposes them in his gospel in the form of a striking contrast of four *Beatitudes* (or 'Blessings') and four *Woes* (or 'Curses') [Lk. 6:20-26]. In both cases (Mt. and Lk.) we are faced with the values of Jesus Christ and his Kingdom of light, truth, justice, peace and love highlighted in stark conflict with the worldly values of the kingdom of darkness, falsehood, oppression, hostility and hatred.

Whether in Matthew's intent of focusing on Jesus as the "new Moses", who from a 'new mountain' (in his *Sermon on the Mount*) proposes, as the long-awaited Messiah and King of the Jews, a 'new' kind of "Law" for the messianic times foretold by the prophets, **or** according to Luke's intent and purpose of portraying Jesus as the Son of Man who reveals the compassionate and gracious, human and humane face of God and brings to *all of humankind* his Father's gift of "salvation", we are able to discern, in very truth, **not** eight "Blessings" (Mt.) **nor** four "Blessings" and four "Curses" (Lk.), but in each of the "Blessings" (Mt. and Lk.) no other "new" standard, rule or law than that of *"handing over self in love"* or *"inner freedom"*; and further, in each of the "Curses" (Lk.), no other norm, standard or criterion than that of "closing self upon self" or "inner bondage".

The fact is that the Saviour's values – should we not rather say, *one single* distinctive value (!) – constitute(s) what we are today calling the unique and only criterion of **Christian spiritual discernment** – namely, that distinctive sign by which we recognise anything or anybody as truly, genuinely and authentically belonging to Jesus Christ and his Spirit. How direly, indeed, do we stand in need of such **spiritual discernment** in a globalised world that has become the worldwide stage and arena of widespread and chaotic confusion of values!!!

Herbert Alphonso SJ

> ## Deepen our understanding of the message of John the Baptist.
> ## Reflect on the demands it makes on us.

[**Note:** *In the Assessment Folder for this module on the DVD there are twenty-two assessment tasks and five assessment sheets mapped to the Bishops' Conference Levels of Attainment in RE, 2007]*

PPP: Starting point John the Baptist.

Explain that thirty years will have passed since the birth of Jesus but he has not yet started his public ministry. God has sent John the Baptist to prepare the way for him.

Song: 'Prepare Ye the Way of the Lord' from the musical 'Godspell' if you have it.

John the Baptist was the fearless, wild preacher. He had the courage, the passion and the vision to prepare the way for Jesus.

Read the text in the Pupil's Book. Draw attention to the images from the scriptural text regarding his appearance, his vegetarian diet, the choice of language he used to speak to the people.

Discuss: John's message is radical. It is a wake-up call to all of us. Why?
Who would we say today challenges us to think of the needs of others? *(Bob Geldof, CAFOD, Pope Benedict XVI, Aid to the Church in Need, etc).* What catching headlines do the prophets of today use? *(Make Poverty History; Live simply so that other can simply live).*

Additional Activities

WS 1 John the Baptist

Assessment Folder:
Assessment sheet: **John the Baptist – Advice** (Guided thinking map)
Assessment task: **John the Baptist.**

Plenary: Ask pupils to write down the most important aspect of the lesson today and, then, to share it with the person next to them. Choose five to share it with the whole class.

Know that Jesus came to show us that He is the Way to the Father. Consider what this means for us.

Starting point:
Before opening the textbooks discuss with pupils:
- what they value in life;
- what value they attach to success;
- what they would like to have most of all;
- what they would do if provoked by others;
- who comes first in their life for them.

Flipchart: Values.

Other Resources Folder:

- **VALUES A & B** for you to use as you think best. You may wish to show Values A to see if and where they compare with the values pupils have shared with you. Then show Values B – the values Jesus gives us.

- Copy of the **BEATITUDES.**

Pause to reflect: Light a candle, darken the room, play very soft music and allow time for pupils to consider their own values and to think of what Jesus would say about them.

PPP: Beatitudes

Activity

The Beatitudes are in this **Pupil's Book** page 43. Pupils could be asked to write their own explanation of one or more of them before they see them in the textbook. Then, using their ICT skills, they could make a poster of one of the beatitudes for display. They could combine their own thoughts with those in the text book and suggest a way to put them into practice.

Plenary: Ask pupils to draw a 'mind map' of three ways Jesus teaches us how to live.

Assessment Folder: Assessment sheet: **The Beatitudes and your values.**

> ### Understand that Jesus came to help all people come close to God. Reflect on how Jesus works through Christians today.

Starting point: Draw on the pupils' prior knowledge of scripture texts by asking them to tell you about some of the things Jesus did to help people. What do these actions tell us about Jesus? What do they tell us about the people who were helped or cured?

Explain to pupils that it is easy to read all the miracles and quickly forget what they tell us. It is a deliberate choice here to only choose a few and to take time to really reflect on them: to be part of the scene, to be a witness and to allow Jesus to speak to us through them. *(Teachers have to make time to do it themselves before they share it with the class otherwise their delivery will not be effective – prayer and reflection are all important).*

Meditation: 'The Son of the Widow of Nain' (Lk. 7: 11-16) could be used for a guided meditation. Create an atmosphere of silence, help pupils to become still, feet on the ground, all books closed, etc.. Invite the pupils to imagine they are a close friend of the boy who was dead or of the mother.

The teacher should read the text slowly together with the commentary on it.
Pause and then make links to situations today.

PPP: 'The Son of the Widow of Nain'.

Let us pray for the mothers who hear that their son or daughter has been killed fighting in war in different parts of the world. Lord, in your mercy comfort these mothers.

Let us pray for parents whose sons or daughters are hooked on drugs and cannot break the habit. Lord, in your mercy comfort these parents.

Let us pray for all who have lost the ones they loved. Lord, give them your comfort and help them to experience your presence in their lives.

Other Resources Folder:
Jesus cures the sick man at the Pool of Bethzatha (Jn. 5:1-18)
Cure of the Centurion's Servant (Lk. 7:1-10)
Background: The centurion was a Roman military officer, captain of a hundred soldiers and disliked by most of the Jews. He understood Jewish customs and he knew that, based on these, he was not worthy for Jesus to enter his house. Yet his **faith** in Jesus was so strong that he only needed a word from him to know that his slave would get better.
He believed that Jesus had power and authority and could do anything.
In the centurion, Jesus saw faith in him, love for his slave and willingness to help the Jewish nation.

Make links: Like the centurion who considered himself unworthy to receive Jesus into his house, at Mass, just before we receive Holy Communion we say: "Lord, I am not worthy to receive you, but only say the word and I shall be healed".

Additional Resource: There is a picture of Jesus, Divine Mercy in the folder 'Other Resources' on the DVD ROM. It may be useful if pupils are making a collage of how Jesus works through other people today.

Starting point: Think of situations or things that we attach a lot of importance to and, instead forget or overlook much more important things. Draw out from pupils, give prompts if necessary, but encourage them to speak freely. Examples might be the importance we attach to the way we look, what we wear, the things we have.

Are we valuing what is all important or are we slaves to fashion?

Of all that we have – what do we really need?

Are we able to spot the pressures?

What pressure do we experience from our peers? Are they right or wrong?

Make links: Jesus wanted to transform Judaism. To do this he challenged, shocked, scandalised and infuriated some people. Let us find out what happened – but let us keep in mind that we too may be caught up in all kinds of things that Jesus wants to challenge us with today. We need to keep in mind that he is always seeking us out if we stray from him – he wants us for himself.

Pupil's Book page 50 - Background: 'Disciples picked corn' (Mk. 2: 23-28).

The bread of Presence was an offering, often of food, made to God by the people in their local shrine. Only the priests who looked after the shrine were allowed to eat the offerings the people left. David broke the law by taking the sacred bread and giving it to his men to eat (Mk. 2: 25).

The Sabbath was a day of rest. Jews must not even prepare and cook food on the Sabbath. No work should be done. Jesus was showing them that their rules matter more than people's needs. He wanted to show that he is the true King but not yet recognised and that he has the right when people are hungry to by-pass the normal regulations. Key point was that Jesus wanted to emphasise the law of love.

Pupil's Book page 51 - Background: 'The woman caught in adultery' (Jn. 8: 3-11).

At the time of Jesus, Jewish society was biased in favour of men. By refusing to condemn this woman and challenging the men who accused her, Jesus was challenging the bias against women in his society.

WS 2 Woman caught in adultery.

Answer to question in Pupil's Book, pages 51-52

   a) If Jesus had said that the woman caught in adultery should be punished, his teaching on forgiveness would become worthless.

   b) If he instructed them not to punish her, they would have said that he is against the Law of Moses.

WS 3 Jesus visits his home town (for more able pupils).

WS 4: Private Eye writing frame to help the less able pupils.

Additional activity:

a) Read about Jesus healing the woman who was crippled on a Sabbath day (Luke 13: 10-17).

b) Why were some people indignant and others delighted?

c) What was the lesson that Jesus wanted them to understand?

Assessment: sheet: 'Jesus and the religious authorities' (Guided thinking map).

**Know that Jesus is truly God and, as a man, truly human.
Reflect on what this means for us.**

Note: *It is of upmost importance for pupils to have a good knowledge of this KLO even though it has not been possible to fit it into the Pupil's Book.*

Background:

In the early Church, there was controversy over the person and natures of Jesus. It was at the Council of Chalcedon in 451 that it was settled that the two natures – human and divine – were in the person of Jesus. This is known as 'the hypostatic union'.

Starting Point: A question of identity – Who is Jesus? Did he experience hunger? Did he experience sadness? Did he get tired and weary? If so, why do we claim that he is God? If he is God, then why did he suffer the same things as we do? This is a mystery; let us try to unravel it.

Flipchart: Jesus: true God and true man.

Explain that the word **INCARNATION** means that God, who is divine, took on human flesh and blood and became a real man. Jesus is not part God and part man; he is not a confused mixture of the divine and the human.

"Jesus became truly man while remaining truly God. Jesus is true God and true Man" (CCC464). It is through Jesus that we can go directly to God and he leads us into a loving relationship with God the Father.

PPP: Jesus true God and true man.

Worksheet in Teacher's Book page 57 **Jesus true God and true Man** (Guided thinking).

WS 5 Jesus is truly God and, as man, truly human (for less able pupils).

WS 6 Mystery of the Incarnation (for more able pupils) also in the Teacher's Book page 58.

🎧 **Audio recording: 'The Mystery of Jesus' on DVD ROM in 'Other Resources' folder.**

ADDITIONAL ACTIVITIES

1. '60 SECOND PRESENTATIONS' Work in pairs.
   a) Pick a scripture reference each, one to show Jesus was truly divine and the other showing his true humanity.
   b) Look up the scripture texts in your Bible and take time to study them carefully.
   c) You have one minute each to present your evidence to the class for claiming that Jesus is truly God and, as man, truly human.

[Note: It will help to have scripture texts cut out and in a box so that all texts will be covered at least once. Use a camcorder to record the presentations.]

2. Why isn't Jesus simply considered a wise man like Socrates? Or a prophet like Muhammad? Or enlightened like Buddha?
Prepare your points for a discussion.
[References for possible websites: Socrates – History for Kids; Islam (Muslim) for Kids; Buddhism: Basic Beliefs or URI Kids-World Religions]

Assessment Folder:
Assessment Sheet: **'The Mystery of the Incarnation'.**
Assessment Task: **Jesus, unique & original.**

> # Understand who Jesus is.
> # Reflect on who He is for us.

Starting point:
The content for this section is best used for reflection. Try to make time and space to allow the words of Jesus to speak to each individual. It could be used as a guided meditation.

Teachers need to respect pupils' freedom to accept or reject the teaching of Jesus. The disciples were very slow to grasp the full significance of what Jesus was teaching them. It was only after the Resurrection that they really began to understand it and it was only when the Holy Spirit came upon them that they had the courage to go out and spread the Good News.

✏️ **WS 7 Living out the teaching of Jesus** (for less able pupils).

✏️ **WS 8 Invitation to the Kingdom** – This can be used for reflection.
a) Why do you think God the Father wants us to do what Jesus tells us?
b) How are these requests likely to influence and change our lives?

✏️ **WS 9: Final plenary** worksheet 'Let us look back on what we have learned'.

> ## Know that Jesus is truly God and, as a man, truly human.
> ## Reflect on what this means for us.

Starting Point:

Think about the months, even years of devoted training by the participants for the Olympics. The sacrifices and efforts they make in an attempt to win a medal and fame for their country. How does that compare with all that God has to offer us if we truly offer our lives to Him?

We are going to reflect on the lives of some people who made the radical choice of not just putting Jesus first in their lives but of Jesus being everything for them. Think again about the words of Pope Benedict XV1:

> "If we let Jesus into our lives, we have lost nothing, nothing, absolutely nothing of what makes life free, beautiful and great. No! Only in this friendship are the doors of life opened wide. Only in this friendship is the great potential of human existence truly revealed. Only in this friendship do we experience beauty and liberation".

It is in the lives of saints that we are taken beyond our daily experience to discover how Jesus works in the hearts and minds of those who seek him.

Flipchart on St. John Vianney: the following questions are to help pupils reflect on what they read in the textbook.

- What command did St. John Vianney believe he was fulfilling?
- Why do you think he wanted to fulfil this command?
- To what extent did he dedicate his life to fulfilling this command?
- What did other people think of him?
- Why do you think so many wanted to go to him for the Sacrament of Confession?
- What did he do when he prayed?
- What do you think about the way he prayed?
- How do you think Jesus felt about it?

Jesus true God and true Man

a) Choose one of these scriptural texts and explain what it reveals about the nature of Jesus.

b) Explain how belief in the divinity and humanity of Jesus may inspire and influence you and others.

Luke 2:5-7
Luke 24:42-43
John 20:22-23
John: 20:8
Mark 15:37

Effects of this believe on:

Me

My family

My friends

This text tells me that the nature of Jesus was:

Human ☐

Divine ☐

Write a summary of the text:

The Mystery of the Incarnation

The word **INCARNATION** means that God, who is divine, took on human flesh and blood and became a real man. This is a mystery and can only be understood by faith. He is not part God and part man; he is not a confused mixture of the divine and the human.

The **Catechism of the Catholic Church** states:

"At the time appointed by God, the only Son of the Father, the eternal Word, that is, the Word and substantial Image of the Father, became incarnate; without losing his divine nature he has assumed human nature" (para. 479).

"Jesus Christ is true God and true man, in the unity of his divine person; for this reason he is the one and only mediator between God and man" (para. 480).

"Jesus Christ possesses two natures, one divine and the other human, not confused, but united in the one person of God's Son" (para. 481).

God reveals Himself to us through Jesus, who is truly God and, as a man, truly human. Through Jesus, we can go directly to God and he leads us into a loving relationship with his Father.

Fully Divine

Jesus had power and authority over nature.
(Mk. 4:35-41 Mt.14:23-33).

Jesus claimed the right to forgive sins.
(Mk. 2:3-12; Jn 20:22-23).

Out of compassion for people's suffering Jesus cured the sick. (Mk 1:32; Mk 2:1-12)

Jesus rose from the dead and appeared to the disciples. Jn. 20:8; Jn. 20:19 Lk. 24:42

Fully Human

Jesus ate food (Lk. 24:42-43)
He got tired (Jn. 4:6).
He needed to sleep (Mt. 8:24).
He wept (Jn. 11:32-37).
He suffered (Lk. 22:41-44).
He died (Mk. 15:37).

Jesus was born of a woman. (Lk. 2:5-7).
He grew and developed physically. (Lk. 2:39).

Activities

1 Take time to think about the scripture texts above.
   a) Choose one that most appeals to you. Look up the reference.
   b) In groups, share your chosen texts and explain how it shows either the humanity or divinity of Jesus.

2. Explain how belief in the divinity and humanity of Jesus may influence you and others. Think about:
   o what makes Jesus human;
   o what he did to help those who were suffering and in trouble;
   o how his attitude to others might inspire and influence you and others;
   o what makes Jesus divine;
   o how he used his power and authority;
   o the effect it had on others;
   o how his actions and words might inspire and influence you and others (AT2 L5 (i)).

3. Choose one of the quotations from the Catechism of the Catholic Church on first page.
   a) Explain what it means in your own words.
   b) Give examples from the scripture texts to support it.

4. The Church

Religious Education Curriculum Directory

"The Church is the family of God, the people that God gathers in the whole world. The Church is the communion of Christ's disciples brought together in Christ its Head by the Holy Spirit. It is the Body of Christ, the Temple of the Spirit. As the People of God, the Church is drawn into Christ's praise of the Father and Christ's mission in the world."

"Christ gave his Church a structure in calling and choosing twelve apostles. With them and their successors he shares his mission, his power and authority. In the coming of the Holy Spirit at Pentecost the Church was revealed and its mission (apostolate) to the nations begun. Through the ministry of the successors of the apostles, the Pope and bishops, the Holy Spirit guides and preserves the Church from error in matters of faith and morals." [Page 19]

Key Learning Objectives

Attainment Targets 1: Learning *about* the Catholic faith.
Attainment Targets 2: Learning *from* the Catholic faith.

- Understand how the Church began.
  o Think about the message it has for us.

- Be aware of some of the challenges the first Christians encountered.
  o Reflect on the challenges we face today as Christians.

- Know that the Church is the People of God.
  o Reflect on what this means for us.

- Understand that the Church is the Body of Christ.
  o Be aware of the commitment that this requires.

- Know some of the history of the early Church.
  o Reflect on what we can learn from it.

- Know that Jesus gave his mission, power and authority to the apostles and through them to the Church today.
  o Think about how we can contribute to the life of the Church.

Theological Notes

4. The Church

[A] The Church as Mystery

In the Creed, we say, "I believe in the Holy Catholic Church". The Church is a mystery of faith. Not rarely do we find Christians – yes, not a few Catholics – for whom the Church is marginal. "Of course, I am part of the Church", we hear them say, "and so what! It does not at all affect my life, my relationships, my professional or social or civic commitments, my daily activity". This is sad, even tragic, when we come across Catholics who openly affirm and, seemingly, take pride in proclaiming: "Jesus Christ, yes; the Church, no! It is Jesus Christ I cling to personally; I'll give my life for him. The Church, for me, is not only peripheral; I wish to have nothing to do with the Church". Such affirmations mean, in the final analysis, that these Catholics have not even understood the mystery of Jesus Christ. One cannot be closely attached to Jesus Christ and his mystery without a close and profound attachment to the Church, the mystery of the Church. To have a profound personalised **sense** of Jesus Christ is to have a profound personalised **sense** of the Church.

The Church, like Jesus Christ, is a *mystery of faith*. Now, as we know, the word "mystery" often connotes something hidden, difficult to fathom, inscrutable, perhaps even exotic. People speak, for example, of the "mysterious" East, the "mysterious" Orient. This is not the sense of "mystery" we are talking about. When speaking of the "mystery" of the Church, Vatican II in **Lumen Gentium** meant something very specific in the rich and deep biblical sense of "mystery" – how very often, for example, St. Paul speaks of the "mystery" hidden before all ages in the Father's bosom, yet revealed in time and manifested in and through his Son Jesus Christ! No wonder, Vatican II's Theological Commission explained mystery as used in **Lumen Gentium** in these words: "a divine, transcendent, salvific reality which has been revealed and manifested in a visible form, even a human form". A "divine transcendent reality", namely, something belonging to the reality of the transcendent God himself; but this reality had not remained just with God. It has been "revealed" for our salvation ("salvific") and "manifested in a visible form", among us human beings.

"Mystery", however, cannot be defined in the sense in which we define something mathematical, something – as we say – belonging to the "exact sciences". This is why the Second Vatican Council (1962-65) stated that the best way to describe the "mystery" of the Church would be to approach it through its rich biblical images. The word of God culls these images at times from the agricultural and pastoral life of a farmer, at other times from the area of construction, building, for example. For our purposes of acquiring and assimilating a profound "sense" of the Church so as to "love" the Church, it would be best to concentrate on three or four appropriate images - namely, the "People of God", the "Body of Christ", the "Spouse/Bride of Christ" or even the "Communion (*koinonia* = common union) in the Spirit". We must note one thing right away: none of these images, taken by itself, suffices to grasp or comprehend the mystery of the Church; they are complementary images, each one offering one or other rich facet of the "mystery" of the Church, but needing to be completed by the others. It would help to remind ourselves that "the Church" is not out there; "**we**" are "the Church": "**we**" are the "People of God", the "Body of Christ", the "Spouse/Bride of Christ", the "Communion in the Spirit".

[B] The Church as "People of God"

Chapter two of **Lumen Gentium** is devoted to this image of the Church as the "People of God".

What are the theological and spiritual depths of this "People of God" image of the Church? This "People of God" is first of all not some altogether new beginning. It is in clear continuity with the People of God with whom God made the covenant on Mt. Sinai: our roots are in the Old Testament, in that people whom God chose and with whom he made his covenant, constituting them as *his own people* (cf. Ex. 19:3-6; 24:1-8). And yet, this "People of God", which is the Church of Jesus Christ, is a *new* People of God; on this *newness* we shall dwell a little later. Further, this "People of God" is "on the move": it is a *pilgrim people*, marching through history, *real* human history – **not** some airy-fairy, dream-world entity – marching forward to the completion and consummation of its mystery as "People of God". It is quite moving to read in that Chapter two of **Lumen Gentium** the various stages, which God in his love prepared from all eternity, of his plan and design for our salvation – the stages of this "mystery of the Church". God first **prefigured** this "mystery" already in creation; then, in a second phase of **preparation**, he prepared "the Church" with the Old Testament "People of God"; later came Jesus Christ who, through some special deeds **actuated** or made actual the setting-up or institution of the **new** "People of God" in clear continuity with the old "People of God". Still later, we have the **public manifestation** or revelation of this "People of God" on the day of Pentecost with the outpouring of the Holy Spirit, when the Church, the new "People of God", was born publicly. This new people, now publicly manifested, begins its ongoing march through history which has not yet finished, because it is moving, says **Lumen Gentium,** towards its **consummation** at the end of time; this will be at the Second Coming of the Lord, when he will come to gather his people and take them on to the fulfilment of the Kingdom.

At this juncture, we need to spell out two important consequences of what we have just exposed of the Church as "People of God". The first is that of facing a very real risk of a distorted modern-day analysis and interpretation of the Church as "People of God". Not a few of our contemporaries approach this biblical reality with a sociological understanding of the term "people" having culled from studies on human society what a "people" is, such of our contemporaries wish to add on to this sociological reality its specifying element: it is not just any "people", but the "People of God". This kind of approach is fraught with serious risks: for it starts with "people" as a sociological reality, to which is added the fact that God enters into this reality, because God chooses it and makes it his own. And so, we have Christians and Catholics today who are spearheading movements, so-called movements of renewal, based on a heavily-accentuated sociological understanding of the mystery of the Church. The fact is that the starting-point is **not** a "people" in the sociological sense; the take-off point is **not** sociological at all. It is **God** who takes the initiative in intervening to set up this group of scattered tribes as a "people" – indeed, **his own people** – by making a covenant with it. Under the saving initiative and primacy of God's love, Moses had got together and led these scattered tribes out of Egypt. The specifying element is clearly, then, *God's initiative of love* and *God's covenant* – **God**, who constitutes those scattered tribes as a people, as *his own* people. Thus it is God who says, "You were no people, now you will be a people, my people, and I will be your God".

Next, is the question of this *new* "People of God" that we have mentioned. In what exactly consists this **newness** of this *new* "People of God" – the "People of God" of the New Testament? We have insisted on the *continuity* of this *new* "People of God" with the Old Testament "People of God". If, then, there is **newness** in the New Testament "People of God", there is also a certain specific *discontinuity* with the Old Testament "People of God". What is this *discontinuity* which makes of the New Testament "People of God" a *new* "People of God"? The answer lies in the **covenant** made by God. God's covenant made at Mt. Sinai was the specifying element that constituted the group of scattered tribes into a "people", God's chosen people, *God's own* people. Now, we know that there is a *new* covenant which God made in and through his Son Jesus Christ; we must underscore, however, **how** God made this *new* covenant, and in what exactly lies its **newness**. Jesus Christ did **not** make it in the blood of a lamb or of any animal; he made it in **his own blood**. This is the whole burden of the Letter to the Hebrews in sharply contrasting the New Testament priesthood of Jesus Christ – the unique and *only* priest of the New Testament, in whom alone all other New Testament priests are priests – with the priesthood of the Old Testament. Whereas the sacrifices offered by the Old Testament priests were sacrifices made in the blood of animals (bulls, goats, calves or lambs) – that is, the offering of something outside of, external to, the priest offering the sacrifice – Jesus Christ did not offer something outside of himself: he shed **his own blood**, he **handed over himself**. So the Old Testament covenant on Mt. Sinai was made in the blood of an animal (cf. Ex. 24:3-8); the New Testament covenant was made in Jesus Christ's own blood (cf. Mt. 26:27-28; Mk. 14:23-24; Lk. 22:20; 1 Cor.11:25). The Letter to the Hebrews underlines the same very strongly in Chapters 9 and 10 (Heb. 9:12; 15.18-20, 24-26; 10:4-10, 19-20). Jesus did not enter into the Holy of Holies once a year, as did the High Priests of the Old Testament with the blood of an animal. Jesus did not pull aside a curtain of canvas to enter the Holy of Holies. He broke open a **new** way through his own flesh, and entered once and for all into the Holy of Holies with **his own blood** – **himself**. In all of **this** lies the **newness** of the *new* "People of God". If we have not grasped **this newness** of the **handing over of ourselves** (**not** of something outside of ourselves), we have not understood at all the depths of the mystery of the Church as the "People of God".

We can, therefore, best close our exposition of the mystery of the Church as "People of God" by citing a very pertinent text from the First Letter of St. Peter: **1 Pet. 2**. This is one of the richest synthesis texts of the whole New Testament. Among its first verses we read these significant words: "Come to him (namely, to Jesus Christ), to that living stone rejected by men, but in God's sight chosen and precious; and you, like living stones, be yourselves built into a spiritual house, to be a holy priesthood, to offer spiritual sacrifices acceptable to God through Jesus Christ" (1 Pet. 2:4-5). So, not only is Jesus Christ priest, temple and sacrifice, but every single Christian is, in and with Jesus Christ, priest and temple and sacrifice. In this precise context it is that St. Peter gives us, in verses 9 and 10, the rich biblical backdrop to contemplating that mystery of the Church as the "People of God": "You, then, are a chosen race, a royal priesthood, a holy nation, God's own people, that you may declare the wonderful deeds of him who called you out of darkness into his marvellous light. Once you were no people, but now you are God's people ..." (1 Pet. 2:9-10). In these words we recognise the *continuity* of the New Testament People of God with that people constituted by God at Mt. Sinai when he made a covenant with them, for we read in the Book of Exodus: "You have seen what I did to the Egyptians, and how I bore you on eagles' wings and brought you to myself. Now, therefore, if you will obey my voice and keep my covenant, you shall be my own possession among all peoples; for all the earth is mine, and you shall be to me a kingdom of priests and a holy nation" (Ex. 19:4-6). But in the passage we have cited from 1 Pet. 2:4-5, we are also given the *distinctive newness* of the

New Testament "People of God" for, in Jesus Christ, priest, temple and sacrifice, every single baptised Christian is priest, temple and sacrifice, offering **spiritual** sacrifices acceptable to God through Jesus Christ. These "spiritual" sacrifices (namely, sacrifices vivified and animated by the Spirit of Jesus Christ) have as their essence what is characteristic of the unique New Testament priest and priesthood – that is, the *handing over of self in love*, not the sacrifices which offered the blood of animals. Doubtless, all of this only confirms us in recognising in the Church as the "People of God" that divine, transcendent, salvific reality revealed and manifested in visible and even human form, which is the deep biblical understanding of "mystery".

[C] The Church as "Body of Christ"

It is St. Paul who, over and over again in his letters, uses this image to speak of the mystery of the Church. However, he uses the image in two distinct ways: one in his so-called "Greater Letters", of which we shall consider two (*Romans* and *1 Corinthians*); and the other in his "Captivity Letters" or letters from prison, like the Letters to the *Ephesians* and to the *Colossians*. In *Romans* and *1 Corinthians* Paul speaks of the "Body of Christ" as applied to *the local Church*: the whole local Church in Rome or in Corinth is the "Body of Christ". In the "Captivity Letters", however, he employs the image of the "Body of Christ" **not** as applied to the local Church: it is *the universal Church* which is the "Body of Christ", and Christ is the Head of the Body. So then, in the case of the "Captivity Letters", the "Body of Christ", which is the universal Church, is like the body's trunk, for Christ is the Head of this Body.

1. *The "Greater Letters": Romans and 1 Corinthians*

In Rom. 12 and 1 Cor. 12, Paul speaks of the Church as the "Body of Christ". We shall take, somewhat in detail, *1 Cor. 12*. This passage can only be understood and interpreted in the context of the division prevailing in the local Church of Corinth. Everybody was claiming charisms, everybody was claiming special gifts of the Spirit. Dealing with this situation, St. Paul admits that the Spirit does give these gifts differently to different persons according to the measure of the Spirit's giving, his liberality, his freedom in giving. There are many gifts, varieties of gifts, but there is **one** Spirit. There are many members, but there is only **one** Body, vivified by **one** Spirit (cf. 1 Cor. 12: 4-13). The sum and substance of Paul's teaching here, in the context of the very real division existing in the local Church of Corinth, is that, just as the human body has different members each of which has a different function while the body remains *one single body*, so in the Body of Christ, which is the Church, there are many gifts given freely by the Spirit, but the Spirit is **one**, and the Church, which is the Body of Christ, is **one**.

In the same context, Paul moves on to suggest that while there are such charisms or gifts which are certainly genuine, perhaps some of the gifts being claimed by some individuals may well not be genuine and authentic. Hence such gifts need to be tested or "discerned"; this test is **love – genuine love** (cf. 1 Cor. 12:27-13:3). Knowing already in his time, as we very well do especially today, that "love" is one of the cheapest words to be bandied about, Paul feels constrained to spell out, from his contemplation of God's way and kind of loving, the qualities of genuine love. Though he enumerates no less than sixteen of these qualities, we realise that he is only offering various expressions of one central quality which he emphasises almost half-way through his list: **"Love does not seek its own interest"** (1 Cor. 13:5). Is this not the characteristic acid-test and touchstone of authentic love? True and genuine love forgets itself, renounces self, gives and surrenders self – in a word, **hands itself over** – that **newness** of the New Testament of which we have spoken earlier.

2. *The "Captivity Letters": Ephesians and Colossians*

Here, too, it will help us to dwell for a while on **Ephesians 4**. We note that this passage is once again written in the context of promoting "union" and "unity": "I, therefore, a prisoner for the Lord, beg you to lead a life worthy of the calling to which you have been called, with all lowliness and meekness, with patience, forbearing one another in love, eager to maintain the unity of the Spirit in the bond of peace. There is one body and one Spirit, just as you were called to one hope that belongs to your call, one Lord, one faith, one baptism, one God and Father of us all, who is above all and through all and in all. But grace is given to each of us according to the measure of Christ's gift" (Eph. 4:1-7).

In the context of such an appeal for 'union' and 'unity', then, Paul comes to speak of the 'Body of Christ': "And his gifts were that some should be apostles, some prophets, some evangelists, some pastors and teachers in roles of service to help make the faithful ready to build up the Body of Christ, till we become one in faith and in the knowledge of God's Son and reach mature personhood in Christ. All this, in such a way that we may no longer be children tossed here and there by every wind of doctrine that originates in human trickery and skill in proposing error. Rather, living and speaking the truth in love, we are to grow up in every way into him who is the Head, into Christ; from him the whole Body grows and, with the proper functioning of the members joined firmly together by each supporting ligament, builds itself up in love" (Eph. 4:11-16).

One immediate reflection on our part, at this stage, is to ask ourselves whether this Pauline image of the mystery of the Church as the "Body of Christ" adds anything to its earlier image as "People of God". We realise that the "People of God" image, by itself, indicates no particularly intimate life-union between God or Christ on the one hand and the Church on the other. But the image of the "Body of Christ" speaks eloquently of the intimate union between Christ (the Head) and the Church (his Body) – such intimate union, in fact, that Christ, as Head, becomes the life-giving, vivifying principle of the Body, the principle that makes life flow into the Body: there is such intimate organic unity between the Head and the members that the Head becomes the living life-principle building up the Body. This is manifest not only in Eph. 4:11-16 which we have cited above; it is once again in evidence in Col. 2:17-19 (where verse 19 is almost a word-for-word repetition of Eph. 4:16**).**

It is interesting to note that Paul attributes to Christ as Head the quality of "governing principle" in the sense of "sovereign power, authority and dominion", as we read explicitly in Eph. 1:20-23 (especially in verse 23). These aspects of "governing principle" and "organic life-giving principle" attributed to Christ as Head are not to be seen as disparate or disjunctive aspects; they are to be synthesised and integrated, as Paul himself makes clear in his marvellous Christological hymn of cosmic sweeping dimensions in his Letter to the Colossians (Col. 1:12-20). In it Paul proclaims that everything that has been created, has been created *in* Christ Jesus, *through* Christ Jesus, *for* Christ Jesus. In other words, Christ Jesus is the <u>Alpha</u> and the <u>Omega</u> of all creation and all re-creation: Not only, "in him all things were created in heaven and on earth ..., *whether thrones or dominions or principalities or authorities*" (Col. 1:16) – that is, he is the "governing principle", but also, "he is the Head of his Body, the Church; the beginning, the first-born from the dead ... in him all the fullness of God was pleased to dwell" (Col. 1:18-19 – that is, the Risen One who is the fullness of life and the source of life: he is the "living and life-giving principle"). **And all this**, "reconciling all things ... making peace **by the blood of his cross**" (Col. 1:20), echoing what is said in Eph. 1:13-16: "in Christ Jesus you who once were far off have been brought near **in the blood of Christ** ... so making peace and **reconciling us to God in one Body through the Cross**" – to paraphrase it equivalently, **all this, by handing himself over in love**.

[D] The Church as "Spouse/Bride of Christ"

We have stressed that the image of the Church as "Body of Christ" clearly accentuates the intimate union between Christ and the Church. The particular risk that the image of the "Body of Christ" carries is that, imperceptibly and without quite realising it, we tend to identify Christ and the Church. It must be quite categorically stated that the Church is **not** Jesus Christ; the Church is the Church of Jesus Christ. This is why the image of the Church as "the Spouse/Bride of Christ" is a wonderful corrective to the risk just mentioned. While there is intimate union between husband and wife, between Bridegroom and Bride, there is a profound person-to-person relationship – a face-to-face relationship – not an identification or fusion between them.

In the very Letter to the Ephesians, after Chapter 4 in which Paul has spoken – as we have seen – of the Church as the "Body of Christ" and Christ, its Head, Paul presents the Church as the "Spouse/Bride of Christ" in Chapter 5: "Husbands, love your wives, as Christ loved the Church and gave himself up for her, that he might sanctify her, having cleansed her by the washing of water with the word, that he might present the Church to himself in splendour, without spot or wrinkle or any such thing, that she might be holy and without blemish. Even so husbands should love their wives as their own bodies. He who loves his wife loves himself. For no man ever hates his own flesh, but nourishes and cherishes it, as Christ does the Church, because we are members of his Body" [it is certainly interesting to note here how the images of the "Body of Christ" and the "Spouse/Bride of Christ" are closely interwoven]. "For this reason a man shall leave his father and mother and be joined to his wife, and the two shall become one. This is a great mystery, and I mean in reference to Christ and the Church" (Eph. 5:25-32). What marvellous words these last ones are in expressing the depth of the theology and spirituality of Christian marriage as portrayed in the intimate relationship between Christ and his Spouse, the Church!

Precious and beautiful as this passage from Eph. 5 is in presenting the Church as the "Spouse/Bride of Christ", it will be extremely helpful to add what St. John has to say, in the same regard, in the Book of Revelation. John describes his vision of a new heaven and a new earth, with the holy city – the new Jerusalem – coming down from God in heaven, clothed as a Bride prepared for her husband; at the same time this *holy city*, this *new Jerusalem*, this "Bride of the Lamb (of God)" is called by God *his dwelling*, *his own people* (cf. Rev. 21:1-3, 9-11)! If in Eph. 5 we had highlighted the interweaving of the images of the Church as "Spouse/Bride of Christ" and as "Body of Christ", here in Rev. 21 we witness the interweaving of the images of the Church as "Spouse/Bride of Christ" and as "People of God". It is, doubtless, highly significant that we are able to trace in the New Testament such a close interweaving of the images of "People", "Body" and "Spouse/Bride" in portraying the mystery of the Church.

Conclusion

What stands out in our approach to the mystery of the Church through the three biblical images we have concentrated on, is that in each of them we contemplate *a divine, transcendent reality, manifested and revealed to us for our salvation in visible, even human, form*. In every single one of them – whether as "People of God" or "Body of Christ" or "Spouse/Bride of Christ" – the Church as "mystery" is never a mere conglomeration of individuals; it is clearly "communitarian", manifestly a "communion" (common union) of persons bonded and knit together by the Spirit of God. If we had wished to focus specifically on the Trinitarian origin and essence of the mystery of the Church, we would have contemplated it in addition as the "Communion (*koinonia*) in the Spirit" – we would then envision the Church as "People of God (**the Father**)", "Body of Christ (**the Son**)" or "Spouse/Bride of Christ (**the Son**) and "Communion in the Spirit (**the Holy Spirit**)".

As we close our theological/spiritual exposition on the Church as "mystery", it is worthwhile underscoring the fact that the Church is a "divine', transcendent reality" – yes, in *visible*, even *human* form! For so many Christians and Catholics the focus is so unilaterally on the visible and human element – indeed, on the all too human and weak element – that they miss out on the divine, transcendent reality; miss out, that is, on the "mystery" which is the Church. Doubtless, the element of "the human", the all *too* human, may at times be scandalous, terribly scandalous! We must never forget that the Word Incarnate, Jesus Christ, was, in his human form, a "scandal" – the word of God says so, when it calls him "a stumbling block" to so many people he met, so much so, that he finished as a "scandal" on the Cross!! The Word of God became flesh, human flesh, *really*; the "likeness of sinful human flesh" are the words used by St. Paul in Rom. 8:3. And yet, we meet and encounter the divine Word of God in this weakness of human flesh: the power of God – the divine, almighty power of God – in the weakness of human flesh! **This** is the "mystery" of faith we believe in: "I believe in Jesus Christ, true God and true man". And together with this: "I believe in the Holy Catholic Church" – yes, a Church of sinners and, yet, a Church that is filled with holiness because of the divine element (the Father through the Son in the Holy Spirit) present and active in it.

Herbert Alphonso SJ.

Additional Suggestions and Resources

> ## Understand how the Church began.
> ## Think about the message it has for us.

NOTE: It will help greatly if you prepare for teaching this module by a) putting out of your mind all the images you have when you think of the word 'church' and, b) read the theological notes in this section as well as the whole text in the Pupil's Book to get a clear understanding of what you are going to cover. There is additional support material on the DVD to help you meet the needs of all abilities.

[In the Assessment Folder for this module on the DVD there are sixteen assessment tasks and four assessment sheets mapped to the Bishops' Conference Levels of Attainment in RE, 2007]

WS 1 Starting point: Research Task in Teacher's Book page 79 and also on DVD. Before discussing anything ask the pupils to write their own explanation of what they think the Church is. Then ask them to take it away and interview six people. Make sure you collect the papers at the next lesson and hold on to them until they have studied the KLO 'Know that the Church is the Body of Christ', Pupil's Book pages 74-77.

PPP: Profile of Peter' is useful for recapping on the character of Peter.

Points for discussion:

Why do you think Jesus asked Peter if he loved him more than the others do? *(On Good Friday, Peter had let him down badly; three times he said he did not even know him when he was asked if he was one of his followers. Jesus wanted to impress on Peter the importance of genuine love.)*

What did Jesus mean when he said: "Feed my lambs"; "Feed my sheep"? *(Jesus knows that he will make Peter head of the Church. So he wanted him to feed his people, that is, to teach, guide, protect, warn of dangers and uplift the downcast. The 'lambs' would be weaker than the 'sheep')*

WS 2 Peter - Character analysis. *(Examples of personal qualities: courageous, fearful, impetuous, insightful, forthright, honest.)*

www.tere.org **Secondary: KS3 Support Material:** click on 'Peter's Progress'.

Audio recording: 'Do You Love Me?' Guided Meditation on DVD ROM in 'Other Resources' folder.

> ┌───┐
> **Understand how the Church began.**
> **Think about the message it has for us.**
> └───┘

Starting Point:
PPP: Disciples – starter.

Flipcharts: Disciples.

Recap on major events in the life of the twelve disciples. They had left everything to follow Jesus.

o What miracles had they witnessed? Who did they think Jesus was?

o Think of the disciples on Palm Sunday when all the people came to welcome Jesus to Jerusalem. They were known as his very close followers. How do you think they felt?

o Cheers quickly turned to jeers – they saw their Lord and Master taken prisoner, scourged and crucified on a cross. Jesus was able to save others but appeared not to be able to save himself. How do you think the disciples were feeling? They fled. Would you blame them? What would you have done?

o Terrified in case the Jewish authorities came for them, they hid in the Upper Room and locked the door. But on the Sabbath morning, the women came rushing to tell them that the tomb was empty. Mary Magdalene told them she has seen the Lord, he had even called her by name. If you had been there what would you have said and done?

o The disciples rushed like excited children to the tomb to find it empty and then Jesus appeared to them, not only once, but several times in different places.

o Where had they seen him? (Road to Emmaus; Upper Room, Sea shore, etc.).

o Jesus reminded them of all he had taught them and explained that he would be going back to His Father and our Father, but he would not leave us orphans but would send His Spirit to be with us always, even to the end of time.

WS 3 'The apostles overwhelmed by events' – Thinking Map

If you have the **DVD** of **Acts show 2:1-4**
This DVD is available from www.paxkom.co.uk or GNN International. Type into Google 'The Visual Bible', the DVD is called 'ACTS' and gives each chapter and verse of the Acts of the Apostle. It is highly recommended and will be useful throughout this module.

Song: 'We thought it was all over', CD Born for This, no. 32 available from publisher CJM, www.cjmmusic.co.uk

Pause to Reflect: Pupil's Book page 66
Peter and John:

o Think of the man lame from birth.
o How does he get to his begging place?
o What frustrations does he experience?
o How do you think people treated him?
o How does he feel about having to look up to people from his position on the ground?
o What is he hoping for from Peter and John?
o Do you think they had money?
o Were they confident that they could act as Jesus did and in His Spirit?
o We know that the authorities were against Jesus so what do you think about Peter and John doing something so AMAZING at the gates of the Temple?
o How do you think the man who was lame felt as the strength came into his ankles and feet?
o What do you think would have been Peter's and John's first reaction?

Flipcharts: Key words.

WS4 'Early Christian Communities' Acts 2:42-47, Pupil's Book page 66

Activity: "God's gifts put man's best dreams to shame", Pupil's Book page 66
(Answer: The man only asked for money – God, working through Peter & John restored his health.)

Assessment Folder for assessment sheet: Early Christians and Christians today

www.tere.org **Interactive: Quick Revision slides:** click on 'The Early Church'

www.tere.org **Secondary: KS3 Support Material:** click on 'Acts Early Church' and 'Church Birth'.

> ## Be aware of the challenges the first Christians encountered.

Starting point:
Pupils record new words and their meaning. Allow a few minutes for them to memorise the meanings. Play: 'Guess my word': a pupil picks a word out of a box and talks about it without saying the word. The rest of the group guess the word as quickly as possible.

'Drama unfolds': Spend time explaining and reflecting on the warning that Jesus had given to the disciples because this is of great importance for what follows. Make links with the advice parents often give to young people today.

The illustration on page 67 depicts Peter's miraculous escape from prison (Acts 12:1-19); the beheading of Paul; the early Christians being fed to the lions in the Coliseum and Christians everywhere who still carry their own cross.

Flipcharts: The Church

DVD Acts 7.51 Show video clip of the **'Stoning of Stephen'.**

Other Resources Folder:

An abridged version of Stephen's speech.

WS 5 Timeline: use Stephen's Speech (Acts 7:1-54), pick out four of the most important events in the history of the Jewish people that you have studied and place them on the timeline in the order in which they occurred.

Quick Quiz Who did Stephen imitate when he forgave those who stoned him? *(Stephen was like Jesus when he forgave those who stoned him. On the cross, Jesus prayed: "Father, forgive them (those crucifying him) for they know not what they do.")*

DVD: Acts 9: 1-7 Show video clip of **Saul's conversion**.

PPP Saul's conversion

By way of introduction, explain that Saul was a very religious Jew and that he believed the teaching of the very early Christians was attacking the Jewish faith.

Assessment Folder: assessment sheet using the picture of Saul's conversion Pupil's Book page 69.

http://www.ainglkiss.com/stories.paul.htm Paul, How you have changed! [Saul on the road to Damascus – for less able pupils]

Video clip Saul: http://uk.youtube.com/watch?v=y4ZJxb4uW-E

Pause To Reflect: (Jesus taught Paul that what he did to his followers he did to Jesus himself. The lesson we can learn from that is that what we do to one another we do to Jesus – we are all members of the Body of Jesus Christ).

DVD: Acts 12: 1-19 Show video clip of Peter's escape from prison.

Activities:

1. Imprisonment of Paul & Silas
Imagine you are the gaoler of the prison. Write a letter to the governor of the prison explaining why you took Paul and Silas home with you.

2. In groups: Choose to be in one of the following scenes:
- o   the apostles arrested and Gamaliel speaking up for them (Acts 5:19-21);
- o   Stephen, the high priest and the Sanhedrin (Acts 7:1-60);
- o   Saul on the road to Damascus (Acts 9:1-19);
- o   Peter arrested and his guards (Acts 12:1-19).

WS 6 Inquiry Brief – Paul; this could also be used for 'HOTSEAT' activity.

WS 7 Peter and Paul (for less able pupils).

Know that the Church is the People of God.
Reflect on what this means for us.

[Plan the Plenary: choose five pupils and tell them that at the end of the lesson you will ask them to come to the front of the class and explain to the others what were the most important aspects of the lesson. On another occasion choose another five].

Starting Point: Invite pupils to give examples of very solemn promises, e.g. Marriage vows. Because we are human beings with human weaknesses, there is always the possibility that promises we make in good faith might be broken.

Explain that when God makes a promise He never breaks it. See if pupils can remember the promise He made to Abraham, to Sarah, to David. Ask pupils if they can remember the **COVENANT** or solemn promise God made to Moses.

PPP Moses the same as for Module 7.2 to explain **COVENANT**.

Explain that a **covenant** is made when the person or people accept the conditions of the promise and undertake to fulfil their part of it. We are now going to see how God has made a **New Covenant** with us in and through Jesus.

Pupil's Book page 72 'Who are we?' St. Peter explains that we are the **Church, the People of God**. We are a people whom God has called "**out of darkness into His wonderful light**". The light that we live in is the knowledge that we have been chosen, loved and owned by Jesus, (1 Peter 2:9).

Activity:
   a) In pairs: pupils read what the early Christians did (Acts 4: 32-35).
   b) Use bullet points to list what the Christians did.
   c) List ways in which we could live like the early Christians:
      • in school;
      • at home.

Explain that a very simple way of living like the early Christians is that instead of thinking all the time of what we want for ourselves, we find ways of putting the needs of others first.

WS 8 People of God = Church (for less able pupils).

Flipcharts: The Church as the People of God.

Develop Thinking Skills in preparation for Activity 3 on page 73 Pupil's Book:
'God has given us our identity so that His identity might shine through us'.
   o What do you think is the first thing we need to be able to do so that God can work through us?
      (If pupils struggle to give an answer ask them to read slowly the text 'Who are we' on page 72 of their Book).
   o In what ways do you think God's identity might shine through us?
      - Remember that to know Jesus is to know God.
      - How can we become like Jesus?
      - What did he do that we can do with his help?
      - What has he asked us to do? Why?

Plenary: Invite the five pupils you chose at the beginning of the lesson to come to the front to explain to the class what they thought were the most important parts of the lesson.

Understand that the Church is the Body of Christ.
Reflect on what this means for us.

Note: The teacher needs to keep uppermost in mind that the Church is the People of God and that it is the Eucharist that makes the Church. These concepts will be difficult and challenging for pupils so extra time needs to be devoted to unpacking them.

Starting Point:

a) Ask the pupils to share with the person next to them what they have learnt about the Church in the last week. Invite feedback from them. If some have failed to grasp that the Church is the People of God, draw on the more able pupils to explain it to them.

b) Discuss some reasons for families or groups for staying together.
   Why do you think it is necessary for the People of God to come together?
   What were the reasons why the early Christians came together? Do those reasons apply to us today?

c) What or who will give us the strength to build a strong community of faith so that we may become true witnesses of Jesus? (Eucharist)

d) Explain that we are now going to deepen our understanding of what it is that gives life, strength and courage to the members of the Church.

WS 9 'Handing over – what does it mean?' This will help to clarify the text on page 75 of the Pupil's Book.

Flipcharts: Handing over.

Flipcharts: Body of Christ.

Prayer:
Lord, be the beginning and end of all that we do and say.
Prompt our actions with your grace,
and complete them with your all-powerful help.
Amen. (Divine Office: Morning Prayer, Week 1)

Pause to Reflect: set the scene with the text in the Pupil's Book page 76 then show
PPP 'Priests' Hiding Holes'.

Activity: Pupils should now receive the 'Research Sheet' they returned to you at the start of this module and do the following activity:

Explain what the Church is and provide evidence to support your beliefs [AT1 L5 (i)].

Peer Assessment: Pupils could check each other's answers to see if they have explained a) Church, the People of God; b) Church, the Body of Christ and what each means in practice.

Plenary: Choose pupils with the best answers to the activity: "Explain what the Church is and provide evidence to support your beliefs".

Know some of the history of the Early Church.
Reflect on what we can learn from it.

Starting Point:

o   Who were the most important people we learnt about so far to whom God chose to reveal himself, to make known his message?

o   Were they always important? Think about each one:
  - Abraham – (had land and was rich – but he was asked to leave everything).
  - David – (was only a young shepherd boy – but trusted completely in God's power).
  - Zechariah – (was a priest in the Temple – but was struck dumb until he learned to completely trust in God).
  - Elizabeth – (was an old woman, well past the age for having a baby and yet God worked through her to bring John the Baptist to us).
  - Mary – (was a young Jewish girl who only desired to do God's will).
  - Apostles – (most of them were fishermen and knew nothing about teaching and preaching).

Now go to the Pupil's Book to discover how and why Christianity spread so quickly.

Activities:
WS 10 'Why did Christianity spread so quickly?'
From a list of reasons, pupils choose the five most important and number them.

PPP The Catacombs – Christians go underground.

PPP Death of the Apostles

PPP Persecution of early Christians

Note: The details on the Power Point presentations of how the apostles died and the persecution of the early Christians are gruesome so teachers need to view them beforehand to see if they are suitable for their pupils.

Assessment Folder for assessment sheet: **Drama unfolds** (links back to page 67 in the Pupil's Book).

WS 11 Quick Quiz

www.tere.org **Secondary: KS3 Support Material:** click on 'Attitudes to Christians.

Useful websites:

[The Ainglkiss websites will help pupils who have difficulty reading the Bible]

www.ainglkiss.com/stories/paul.htm = Paul, How You Have Changed!

www.ainglkiss.com/stories/psj.htm = Paul and Silas in Jail.

www.ainglkiss.com/stories/up.htm = Get Up, Aeneas!

www.ainglkiss.com/stories/dor.htm = Dorcas, the Seamstress.

www.ainglkiss.com/stories/boy.htm = A Boy Saves Paul.

www.ainglkiss.com/stories/ship.htm = Shipwrecked.

http://gardenofpraise.com/bibles.htm = Stories of the Early Church & the Travels of the Apostle Paul.

**Know that the mission, power and authority that Jesus gave to the apostles have been handed on to the Church today.
Think about the impact this had on your life.**

Note: The aim in this section of the module is to give pupils an opportunity to deepen their knowledge and understanding of what happens in their diocese and parish and to consider their role.

Starting point:

a) Recap on the major points you have covered in this module and try to enable pupils to understand where they are in the story of Salvation – see overview 'The Big Picture'.

b) Help pupils to make connections with their own diocese and parish.

Note: This is an activity-based section and each teacher will approach it in his or her own way.

Flipcharts: Mission, Power and Authority passed on to the Church.

Activities in Pupil's Book page 82

Remind pupils to collect a newsletter from their parish church on Sunday. Have some spare copies of newsletters for those who forget.

If pupils do the following activity in the Pupil's Book, you will need to prepare the parish priest in advance so that their letter will be acknowledged.

Discuss what you could do to contribute to the life of your parish. Decide on one or two definite things and as a group write to your parish priest to present your proposals.

WS 12: Island Game & Description of the Island

Assessment Folder assessment sheet: **The Ship of Peter** (for gifted and talented pupils).

www.tere.org: **Secondary: KS3 Support Material** Click on each of the following for a variety of helpful resources:

- o Church Brainstorm;
- o Church Brainstorm (2);
- o Church Layout;
- o Communion of Saints;
- o Organisation in the Church;
- o Pope and Bishops;
- o The Catholic Church Today.

WS 13 Project on parish church:

For additional help see worksheet on www.tere.org Support material - 'Church Layout'.

WS 14 Youth of the Church (for less able pupils).

WS 15 Ordination and role of a bishop.

The Church

Research Task

Ask six people to explain to you what the Church is.

a) First write your own explanation in Box 1.

b) Ask two pupils, two people that are middle-aged and two that are retired. Make sure that at least three of them are Catholics. Put their approximate age in brackets.

c) Write down what each person says. When finished, give it to your teacher.

Your Name:.......................................

1.

2.

3.

4.

5.

6.

7.

Bishop John Han Dingxiang in China
The <u>hope</u> that <u>never</u> dies

Partially concealed in the shrubbery a camera zooms in on the fourth floor of a police block.

Suddenly, the familiar face of Bishop John Han appears at the window. A door opens and he steps out onto the balcony.

Even here he is not free – around the balcony is a cage and he clings to the bars for support.

Dramatically he unfurls a banner proclaiming a message of hope. He knows the camera is there. In his right hand is a cross which he holds and tries to put through the bars over his head.

In 2007, even when he was dying, the authorities in China insisted that there should be nobody from the Church at his bedside. After he passed away, his remains were cremated and his ashes were taken by night to a public cemetery.

He had spent over thirty years in prison but would never give up his faith.
The authorities even controlled the number of people who could visit his grave.

Bishop Han is just one of the many clergy and faithful people who are in prison for their beliefs. One priest has asked: "The best thing you can do is to pray. Please pray that we won't lose faith; that we won't give up trusting in God".

Tasks

1. Why do you think Bishop John Han risked coming out onto the balcony?

2. Why do you think the authorities refused to let members of the Catholic Church come to his bedside when he was dying?

3. What reasons do you think the authorities had for keeping him in prison? Were they justified in doing so? Give more than one point of view.

4. What can we learn from him?

5. Sacraments

Religious Education Curriculum Directory

"A sacramental celebration is woven from signs and symbols which are drawn from the material creation and human culture. In the Church's liturgy they are raised to a new level and become signs of grace of all the new creation in Jesus Christ. The seven sacraments touch all the stages and all the important moments of Christian life."

"In Baptism we are reborn as children of God in Christ and enlightened by the Holy Spirit ...."

"Reconciliation makes sacramentally present Jesus' call to conversion, involves contrition for our sins, confession of them to a priest, and absolution spoken by the priest in the name of Jesus Christ. In the celebration of the sacrament we acknowledge (confess) God's holiness and mercy and are reconciled to God and the community of the Church."

"The Anointing of the Sick makes sacramentally present the compassion and healing power of Christ through the laying on of hands and anointing with oil." [Page 24].

Key Learning Objectives

Attainment Targets 1: Learning *about* the Catholic faith.
Attainment Targets 2: Learning *from* the Catholic faith.

- Deepen our understanding of the sacraments.
  - o Reflect on how they relate to our human growth.

- Understand what the Sacrament of Baptism is and how it happens.
  - o Reflect on what it does for us.

- Reflect on how Jesus explains God's unconditional love for us.
  - o Reflect on what it teaches us about God.

- Understand the Sacrament of Reconciliation;
  - o Reflect on what it does for us.

- Know that Jesus has great compassion and love for all who are sick.
  - o Reflect on what this means for us.

- Know about the Sacrament of the Sick.
  - o Reflect on how it can help us.

Theological Notes

Sacraments

In the earlier "Theological Notes for Teachers" in this book we have seen that in the "mystery of Jesus Christ" there is something profoundly sacramental. We can, in fact, call Jesus Christ the "radical sacrament" of God. When we study the Catechism, we are given the definition of a sacrament as "an efficacious sign of grace", meaning *a visible sign which signifies and effects grace* – a divine reality. This is true, of course. But we realise also today that, while it is correct, this definition offers an abstract kind of understanding of what a "sacrament" is. Today we prefer to express it, theologically and spiritually, in existential and interpersonal terms: a **Sacrament**, we are saying, **is the place of the interpersonal encounter between the Risen Christ who lives and acts in his Church and the person(s) receiving this sacrament**.

In the person of Jesus Christ, true God and true Man, such an interpersonal encounter between God and human beings is realised radically and profoundly – so profoundly and radically that, *in one and the same Person*, we have the meeting or encounter between God and human beings. Jesus Christ is, in fact, the sacrament of the encounter between God and human beings (see Edward Schillebeeckx's book: <u>Christ, the sacrament of the encounter between God and man</u>). In this sense, Jesus Christ is the "radical" sacrament (that is, **the** Christian sacrament, at its very roots). If so, the "mystery" of the Church, as the continuation and prolongation of the "mystery" of Jesus Christ, is itself a "sacrament". Over and over again Vatican II, in several of its documents, calls the Church the "sacrament of salvation". In other words, the interpersonal encounter between God and the human, of which we have been speaking, is now realised in the "mystery" of the Church.

The Church is "sacrament". What we call the "seven sacraments" are the unfolding or externalisation, in seven different ways or forms called "sacraments" of what the Church is in its profound reality and "mystery". In other words, the Church expresses its deep "sacramental" reality in seven different forms called "sacraments" – seven forms that are very closely related to the stages of human growth, growth towards adulthood and maturity. In reaching out to us with his wonderful, providential and caring love, God has always sought, with his exquisite kind of loving, to adapt himself to our human categories – in this case, to adapt himself to the process of human growth and maturing. The seven sacraments touch, in fact, the most important moments and stages of the life of a Christian. Thanks to them, the Christian life of faith is born and grows; it receives healing and the gift of mission. We have, in this way, the three sacraments of Christian initiation (Baptism, Confirmation, Eucharist); then, the sacraments of healing (Reconciliation, Anointing of the Sick); and finally, the sacraments of the service of communion and of mission (Holy Orders, Marriage). These seven sacraments of the Church form a kind of unified organism, in which each one of the seven plays a vital role. In this compact organism of the Church's sacraments, the Eucharist has a unique and central role – we may term it the "Sacrament of the sacraments". The Eucharist is at the very heart of the Church's seven sacraments; indeed, it is at the very heart of the "mystery" of the Church.

The Eucharistic Mystery and the Mystery of the Church

It is from the Eucharist that every other sacrament of the Church's seven distinct sacraments draws its meaning, its full reality, its power. Not only does the Church make the Eucharist; it is, also, the Eucharist that makes the Church. The "Church" and the "Eucharist" are profoundly and organically interrelated.

The Church cannot be the Church without the Eucharist. History is splendidly eloquent on this point. At times of persecution, when the Church was being sought out by her enemies in order to be wiped out and driven into extinction, she earnestly looked out for, and found, extremely unlikely places to celebrate the Eucharist, because she cannot exist without the Eucharist. When the Roman emperors of old violently persecuted the Christians and were bent on stifling the Church out of existence, the Church went underground into the catacombs to celebrate the Eucharist, so that she could live – for, without the Eucharist, the Church could not, and cannot, live or exist or survive; without the Eucharist, the Church cannot be Church.

It is, therefore, not only the Church that makes the Eucharist; it is, as well, the Eucharist that makes the Church – very much and very profoundly so. To deepen our awareness of this, we shall be helped by two brief and very pertinent passages from St. Paul's First Letter to the Corinthians: 1 Cor. 10:16-17 and 1 Cor. 11:23-24. Both these passages focus on the central significance and role of the Eucharist in Christian life and living.

a) 1 Cor. 10:16-17

Here Paul is speaking of the Corinthian Christians' taking part in the pagan sacrifices and their ensuing sacrificial meals. In this context, he says: "The cup of blessing which we bless, is it not a participation in the blood of Christ? The bread which we break, is it not a participation in the body of Christ? Because there is one bread, we who are many are one body, for we all partake of the one bread" (1 Cor. 10:16-17). Paul's profound theological-spiritual message here is as follows: the celebration of the Eucharist is a real participation in the body of Christ – the real body of Christ under the species of bread. But because the bread of the Eucharist is only one real "body of Christ", we who partake of it, though we are many in number, are the one real body of Jesus Christ, which is **both** the Eucharist in its sacramental form under the species of bread **and** the Church in its mystical or "mystery" form of being one "Body" made up of many members. This is a wondrously profound way in which Paul is communicating to us that "the Eucharist makes the Church", helping us to sound the depths of the Eucharistic mystery in its close organic relationship to the mystery of the Church.

b) 1 Cor. 11:23-24

This passage forms part of St. Paul's account of the institution of the Eucharist. Here is what Paul really said to the Corinthians, according to his original Greek text: "For I received from the Lord what I also **handed over** to you, that the Lord Jesus on the night when he was **handed over** (that is, in betrayal) took bread, and when he had given thanks, he broke it, and said, 'This is my body which is **handed over** for you. Do this in remembrance of me'" (1 Cor.11:23-24). We surely note the repeated words "**handed over**" (the Greek verb *paradidomi*). When Jesus was "handed over" in a betrayal of love, he responded by taking bread, giving thanks, breaking it and saying, "This is my body which is 'handed over' (in an ecstasy of love) for you." The repetition of "handed over" is no mere play on words. Paul, passionate lover of Jesus Christ, inspired by the Spirit, gives us the singularly deep meaning of the Eucharist.

We are all aware that the Eucharist is a very rich reality. We need only read what St. John tells us in Chapter 6 of his Gospel, when Jesus is promising the Eucharist in his "discourse on the bread of life" (Jn. 6:32-58 – esp. vv. 51-58), to become freshly aware of the many rich aspects of the Eucharist: it is a real meal, a sacrificial meal; it is a sacrifice of expiation; it is a memorial sacrifice; it is a covenant sacrifice. So many rich realities! Yet none of them is really understood or grasped unless we understand the central point that Paul is communicating to us in the name of God: namely, that the crucial, profound meaning of the Eucharist is 'the handing over of self'. Here it is that we understand what kind of "meal" the Eucharist is, what kind of "sacrifice of expiation", what kind of "memorial" and "covenant sacrifice" it is. All of these are really understood only as animated from within by this inspiring soul of the "handing over of self". How we tend, how easily we are prone, to water down the deep realism of the word of God! For example, is it not true that we interpret the words given here by St. Paul, "Do this in remembrance of me", as meaning merely, "Consecrate bread and wine in remembrance of me"? No, this is **not** merely what Jesus meant. Paul is saying very clearly: Jesus meant, "Do this, which I have done, in remembrance of me" – that is, "*Hand over yourselves.*" <u>This</u> is the "memorial" sacrifice. A "remembrance" not merely in the mind, but a "remembrance" and "memorial" in action (the force of the Greek word, **anamnesis**): truly **handing over yourselves, as I handed over myself** – that is, **handing over self in love**.

This is the depth of the Eucharist. <u>This</u> is how, in real depth, *both* the Church actually makes the Eucharist, *and* the Eucharist actually makes the Church. For, in handing over ourselves in love, we are able, in openness and inner freedom, to become deeply united with Christ and, in him, to become deeply united with one another. We become one in Christ, we become the "Church", the "Body of Christ". When we spoke of the Church's mystery as the "People of God", we saw that the **newness** of this new "People of God" lay in the fact that Jesus did not take the blood of an animal to offer sacrifice; he took his own blood – himself –, made a covenant in his own blood; thus in handing over himself in love, he formed the **new** "People of God". **The body of Christ handed over in love!** This is how the body of Christ remains for ever, the body eternalised in the act of handing itself over. This is how it remains even in heaven: in the Book of Revelation, St. John sees the Lamb around the throne of God, "the Lamb as slain" (Rev. 5:6), the *Lamb as handed over*. This word "handed over" (*paradidomi* in Greek) is one of the favourite words of St. Paul when he contemplates the mystery of Christ and Christ's way of loving (c.f. Eph. 5:2.25). When he shares with the Galatians how much Christ has loved him, he proclaims: "He loved <u>me</u> and *handed over himself* for <u>me</u>." (Gal. 2:20). Not by chance does Paul keep repeating this phrase, "handed over". It is that he has grasped in a deeply personal way the centrality of being a genuine disciple of Jesus Christ, of being a **Christian** – indeed, the centrality of being "Church". We <u>are</u> the "Church", and we live the mystery of the Church when, with Jesus Christ, in Jesus Christ and through Jesus Christ, we "hand over" ourselves in love.

Jesus remains perpetually in the Eucharist in his act of handing himself over in love. How many Catholics have the idea that Jesus is and remains present in the Blessed Sacrament (in the tabernacles of our churches) as at any moment of his life and existence! Not so at all! Jesus remains present in our tabernacles as he becomes present under the species of bread and wine during our celebration of the Eucharist – that is, in his act of handing himself over in love. Did we not read in St. Paul's account of the institution of the Eucharist, "On the night he was *handed over* (in a betrayal of love), he took bread, broke it, and said, 'This is my body *handed over* for you'" (1 Cor.11:23-24)? Jesus, then, remains present in the Blessed Sacrament in this, his handing self over in love. When we "visit" Jesus present in the Blessed Sacrament, we meet and encounter *this* Jesus in his act of "handing over self in love": we actually go to get strength for our daily handing over self in love from the real presence of Jesus' "body handed over in love". Only in this way are we truly the "Body of Jesus Christ" which is the Church. Thus it is that we live in truth the mystery of the Church that we are.

Again, when we speak of receiving "Holy Communion" at Mass – have we really grasped its meaning? Perhaps, a phrase like "receiving holy communion" makes us miss out on the true depths of communion and what we mean, or ought to mean, by that much-used phrase of "receiving communion". By itself, the word "communion" means fellowship; it means "becoming one" (= common union). When I "hand over myself" – forgetting and getting out of myself, my self-love, my self-will, my self-interest – then it is that I am in "communion", because I am open to others. If others have the same attitude towards me, then they are in "communion" with me. This is the mystery of "communion". The Eucharist, then, the heart of which is "handing self over", is essentially a "mystery" of communion. In a very real sense, therefore, we do not receive communion; we receive the "mystery of communion", the heart and nucleus of which is the "handing over of self in love". We receive "Jesus in his handing-over-of-self in love" (this is how he is present under the species of bread and wine), to feed, nourish and strengthen us for our daily handing-over-of-self in love. When Jesus handed himself over in love, he – the Risen Jesus – became the life-giving Spirit open to everybody else, not closed in on himself; he became, that is, the mystery of communion. It is in receiving this Jesus that we are empowered and enabled to become and be the handed-over Body of Christ in our daily life, activity and ministry – to become and be, ever more deeply, the "Church".

Herbert Alphonso SJ

Additional Theological Notes:

Original Sin
Essential Truth Of Catholic Faith

The Catholic doctrine on 'original sin' is, as it were, the 'correlative' or 'counterpart' of the Good News that Jesus Christ is the Saviour of all men and women, that all are in need of salvation and that this salvation is offered to all human beings thanks to Jesus Christ (see Rom. 5:12-21). We firmly believe that any weakening in our acceptance of what divine revelation teaches us on 'original sin' would involve a corresponding undermining of the salvific and redemptive mystery of Jesus Christ.

God created man and woman out of love. He created them in a state of holiness or righteousness, which means, in a relationship of friendship with Him: and God who created them in His image and likeness gave them the gift of 'freedom' or liberty, so that they could *freely* choose to be who they really were, namely 'creatures' of God their 'Creator'. In other words, God wanted them, because He loved them, to *freely* be and live in friendship with Him.

This was God's loving plan not only for Adam and Eve but, inasmuch as they were the 'first parents' of all humankind, also for all men and women after them – for all members of the human race. Such a 'unity' of the entire human race – or 'solidarity' of all human beings – is part of God's loving plan for all of humankind.

However, from the very dawn of history, man and woman were tempted by the Evil One. They misused their God-given gift of 'freedom' to turn against their Creator: they sought to find their self-fulfilment apart from God and from His plan for their life of friendship and happiness with Him.

By this turning against God, Adam and Eve lost their original state of righteousness or relationship of friendship with God. And since God had intended His original plan of friendship with Him for all human beings in and through their 'first parents' Adam and Eve – in virtue of what we have called above the 'unity' or 'solidarity' of the entire human race – so, by their turning against God, Adam and Eve lost that original state of friendship with God for all human beings coming after them. In this sense, Adam and Eve passed on to their descendants in the human race their "human nature wounded by their 'first sin'" and therefore deprived of the original state of righteousness or friendship with God. **This deprivation of the original state of friendship with God is called *original sin*.**

We have just said that ***original sin*** was passed on to all members of the human race – to all, except to Our Lady, the Blessed Virgin Mary who, by a special privilege in virtue of the victory that Jesus Christ to be born of her would win through His death and resurrection over the powers of sin and death, was preserved from this deprivation or 'taint' of *original sin*. This privilege, which we call Our Lady's 'Immaculate Conception', was granted her by God in view of her very specially close and intimate association with her Son Jesus Christ in his entire mystery of redeeming us as our Saviour.

What deprivation called *'original sin'* implies is that our human nature is wounded and weakened, submitted to a 'darkening of the mind' or 'ignorance', also subject to suffering, to the powers and forces of 'death', to an innate inclination or tendency towards 'sin' – this tendency is termed 'concupiscence'.

While all such 'woundedness' and weakening of our human nature does **not** by itself amount to culpable fault or sin, we must never forget that the victory won by Jesus Christ through his paschal mystery of passion, death and resurrection has obtained for us benefits and gifts far superior to those of which we were deprived through the *original sin* of our 'first parents'. For "where sin abounded, graced has abounded all the more" (Rom 5:20). We Christians see the world as created and sustained in existence by the love of God, its Creator; this world, through man and woman, fell into the bondage of sin, but God's redeeming love has freed it from this slavery and transformed it anew in and through the crucifixion, death and resurrection of Jesus Christ His Son, who, in this way, broke the stranglehold of the Evil One over it.

Fr. Herbert Alphonso SJ

Additional Suggestions and Resources

> ### Know what the Sacraments are.
> ### Reflect on how they can help us.

Note: This is probably the most challenging module in this book because a) when you read the theological notes and then read the text in the Pupil's Book you will see that we have simplified it in an effort to make the sacraments meaningful to pupils and b) as a teacher, you will be challenged with questions, such as: 'Why do we need to study the sacraments? What do they do for us? What will we get out of them?' An in-depth study of these theological notes will help together with your own personal reflection, before attempting to teach the module.

There will be a module on the Mystery of the Eucharist in the next book in this series 'The Truth'. However, when you are explaining to pupils the importance of being very conscious of what is happening when we go to the Eucharist and receive the Blessed Sacrament it may help to quote Mother Teresa of Calcutta: "Each time we receive Jesus in Holy Communion he is really and truly present. But if we don't take notice of HIM and let our thoughts wander as soon as we have received HIM, he won't drag us by force to give us his love and help." It is only with his love and help that we will be able to recognise him and discover ways of reaching out to help others.

Starting Point: Pupil's Book: 'Do you have the answers?' Explain to pupils the importance of being able to articulate what their Christian beliefs are and why they hold them. We live in a multi-faith society and it is an essential part of our Christian witness to be able to speak coherently about our faith among ourselves in the Church and to the wider world today.

Flipcharts: Original Sin.

PPP 'Signs & Symbols' – This is just to explain their purpose.

WS 1: 'Effects of the Sacraments' diagram for pupils to complete.

Additional activities:

Think of a word that will help you to remember the names of the sacraments, e.g.
CHAMBER; C=Confirmation; H=Holy Orders; A=Anointing of the Sick; M=Matrimony;
B=Baptism; E=Eucharist; R=Reconciliation.

Sacraments of Christian Initiation:

"The sacraments of Christian initiation – Baptism, Confirmation and the Eucharist – lay the *foundations* of every Christian life. 'The sharing in the divine nature given to people through the grace of Christ bears a certain likeness to the origin, development and nourishing of natural life. The faithful are born anew by Baptism, strengthened by the sacrament of Confirmation, and receive in the Eucharist the food of eternal life'" (CCC para. 1212).

PPP 'Sacraments of Initiation'.

WS 2 'Tuning in'.

WS 3 'Sacrament linked to life'.

WS 4 Sacraments - Links to Eucharist (bubble map).

Flipcharts: Sacraments linked to life.

www.tere.org **Secondary: KS3 Support Material:** click on 'Introduction to the Sacraments'.

> ## Understand what the Sacrament of Baptism is,
> ## how it happens and what it does for us.

Starting Point:

In pairs, pupils think of examples to explain the difference between the physical and the spiritual aspects of our life. *(Example: we need to eat to nourish our physical life. We need to pray to God for strength for our spiritual life.)*

Flipcharts: Physical & spiritual needs – how they differ and their importance.

www.tere.org: Interactive Section: Key Stage 3: 'Sacrament of Baptism'

www.tere.org Secondary: KS3 Support Material: click on 'Rite of Infant Baptism'.

WS 5 Baptism - Signs & symbols (Less able)

WS 6 My Baptism – What happened (Less able)

WS 7 My Baptism Record (Less able)

WS 8 Baptism of Jesus (More able – extension)

Explain: 'imprints an indelible spiritual mark'.
The indelible mark means it cannot be removed. It is a sign that the person belongs to Jesus. If the person remains faithful to his/her baptismal promises he/she will depart from this life marked with the sign of faith.

Prayer Service: based on the **Baptismal Promises,** Teacher's Book page 93.

Deepen our understanding of the Sacrament of Reconciliation. Reflect on how it can help us to grow in our relationships.

Starter activity: There are many temptations for young people today. List some of them.

Starting Point:
Explain to pupils that the parable of the Lost Son is an example of what can happen when a person thinks only of themselves with no thought for others.

Also, we need to remember there is a bit of the Pharisee in each one of us. We can all be self-righteous and judge others according to how we see and understand a situation.

Note: Pupil's Book page 94 Read the Parable of the Lost Son (Lk. 15: 1-3), it will help if the teacher reads these verses aloud or chooses a competent reader to do so.

Activity
Ask the pupils to work in pairs for five minutes to think of similar situations that might arise with young people today.

When pupils feedback, make a note of the most typical examples which you can use in the Reflection Activity on the next page.

Flipcharts: 'Prodigal Son' – The Way Back.

WS 9 The Way Back – use if you do not have access to Interactive Whiteboard. Cut cut up the strips. Pupils have to place the story on the 'Path' in as 'best fit'. They can then check the order from your master copy.

Reflective activity:

a) Help pupils to reflect on what we can learn from **'The Way Back'**.

b) Study **'STEPS TO RECOVERY'** Pupil's Book page 98.

c) Work in pairs or small groups to plan a role-play of one of the most typical examples that pupils gave of a similar situation to the story of the 'Lost Son'. They must now emphasise the 'Steps to Recovery'.

PPP Pope Benedict XVI: Sacrament of Reconciliation

WS 10 'Steps to Recovery for Us'. This worksheet could also be used for silent reflection: **'Conscious Examen'**: that is, consciously to think about what has happened and how we have responded to events.

Also, encourage pupils to make time each night to reflect on what they have done during the day and if they have done something wrong to go through the a), b) and c) of the 'Steps to Recovery'.

This does not replace the Sacrament of Reconciliation; rather, it is a daily practice which helps to give us inner peace.

PPP The Prodigal Son
PPP The Lost Son (for less able pupils)

Additional activities:

1. Start by giving pupils water soluble ink pens.
    a) Invite pupils to write out the things they have done for which they would like to receive forgiveness. Each goes up and puts their paper into a bowl of water. What they have written will be washed away.
    b) Pupils explain the similarities and differences between what they have just done and the Sacrament of Reconciliation.

2. Imagine your school has invited an artist to paint a picture of the parable of the Prodigal Son. What instructions would you want to give to the artist so that he/she would highlight the important parts of the story?

3. Imagine that a friend who is not a Catholic has asked you to explain what the Sacrament of Reconciliation is about. Write down what you would say.

4. WS 11 'Gifts from God – Sin damages the gifts' (Less able).

Extension activities: (More able)

5. CS Lewis said: "There are only two kinds of people, those who say to God, 'Thy will be done' and those to whom God says, 'All right, then, have it your own way'."
   Write a character profile for each of these people. Think of the following:
   - what they do to strengthen their inner lives;
   - where they seek strength and courage;
   - who they turn to when they need help;
   - what they do when they are hurtful to others;
   - what they do when others hurt them;
   - who they give credit to when all goes well.

6. If you truly believe in Jesus and his teaching you must never carry a knife.
   a) Say what you think and why.
   b) Give a different point of view and say why some people hold it.
   c) Say why you disagree with it.
   d) Quote source of evidence from the teaching of Jesus.

Prayer: An Act of Contrition

Oh my God,
because you are so good,
I am very sorry that I have sinned against you,
and, by the help of your grace,
I will not sin again.

Other Resources Folder: Guided Meditation – 'Opening our hearts to Jesus' - this meditation may help to encourage pupils to receive the Sacrament of Reconciliation'.

Prayer

"Lord, make me a channel of your peace.
Where there is hatred,
let me bring your love.
Where there is injury,
your pardon, Lord.
And where there's doubt,
true faith in you."

St. Francis of Assisi

www.tere.org **Secondary: KS3 Support Material:** click on the following for a variety of worksheets:

- o 'Peace in our World';
- o 'As we forgive those ...';
- o 'Sin Forgiveness';
- o 'The Mercy of God'.

Know that Jesus has great compassion and love for all who are sick. Reflect on what this means for us.

Starting Point:

Invite pupils to recall the miracles Jesus worked for those who were ill. What did he require of these people? (Faith)

Additional Activities

1. WS 12 Choose one of the miracles.
   a) Write an eyewitness account of what happened.
   b) Say how it has affected you and your life.

2. There are many miracles today that are never broadcast.
   a) Talk to your parents, relatives or friends to see if they can recall a miracle that has happened to them or someone they know.
   b) Write a report on what they say.

3. Try to put together a class album of '**Miracles in Our Time**'.
   Use a variety of symbols and images to illustrate your story.

Know about the Sacrament of the Sick. Reflect on how it can help us.

Starting Point: Pupils have a few minutes to check that they understand the meaning of all the key words on the Flipchart or Pupil's Book, then play 'Just a minute': A pupil selects a word from the board and talks about it for a minute.

Discuss: 'The True Story'

- o How do you think Peggy may have felt being the only Catholic on the ward?
- o How would you have felt?
- o What temptations might a person experience if they were the only Catholic?

o   How could we overcome such temptations

o   Think about what it means to you to be able to receive Holy Communion.
    (Pause for silent reflection. Invite pupils to share their thoughts with Jesus).

o   After Holy Communion Mrs. O'Hara shared her thoughts with Peggy.
    How do you think Peggy felt?

o   When Mrs. O'Hara was told that the doctors could do no more for her – what was it that
    helped her most of all? How do you know?

o   What can we do to help people who are ill?

o   Faith is not like switching on a mobile phone – we have to continually ask God to
    increase our faith in Him. What steps can we take to help our faith grow?
    (Look back to the Sacraments for help).

Reflection: The Sacrament of the Sick poem, Teacher's Book page 94.

Origin of the Sacrament of the Sick – St. James tell us:
"If one of you is ill, he should send for the elders of the church, and they must anoint him with
oil in the name of the Lord and pray over him. The prayer of the faithful will save the sick
person and the Lord will raise him up again; and if he has committed any sins, he will be
forgiven" (Letter of James 5: 13-15).

**What is the difference between the Sacrament of the Sick and the Last Rites or
Extreme Unction?**

The Sacrament of the Sick can be given to anyone who suffers from serious illness and
infirmity. It is also given to those on the point of departing from this life and was often called
'Extreme Unction'.

"In addition to the Anointing of the Sick, the Church offers those who are about to leave this
life the Eucharist as viaticum. Communion in the body and blood of Christ, received at this
moment of 'passing over' to the Father, has a particular significance and importance. It is the
seed of eternal life and the power of resurrection, according to the words of the Lord: 'He who
eats my flesh and drinks my blood has eternal life, and I will raise him up at the last day'."
(CCC para. 1524).

www.tere.org **Secondary: KS3 Support Material:** click on 'Sacraments of Healing'.

www.albany.edu/~ka762934/anointsick.html A very helpful site with picture of the Sacrament
of the Sick.

Baptismal Promises Ceremony

We reflect in silence for a few moments asking God for the grace to renew our baptismal promises.

Celebrant: Do you reject Satan?
All: *I do*

C.   And all his works?
A.   *I do*

C.   And all his empty promises?
A.   *I do*

C.   Do you believe in God, the Father almighty,
         creator of heaven and earth?
A.   *I do*

C.   Do you believe in Jesus Christ, his only Son, our Lord,
         who was born of the Virgin Mary, was crucified, died, and
         was buried, rose from the dead, and is now seated at the
         right hand of the Father?
A.   *I do*

C.   Do you believe in the Holy Spirit, the holy Catholic
         Church, the communion of saints, the forgiveness of sins,
         the resurrection of the body, and life everlasting?
A.   *I do*

C.   This is our faith. This is the faith of the Church.
         We are proud to profess it, in Christ Jesus our Lord.

TASKS

   a)   **Explain the meaning of the Baptismal Promises.**

   b)   **Why do you think these promises are an essential part of the
        ceremony for a person receiving the Sacrament of Baptism?**

   c)   **Make a summary of the beliefs of a baptised person.**

The Sacrament Of The Sick

How pale my grandmother seemed
as she lay in that bed.
How gently the priest reached out
and placed hands on her head.

My mother explained that
his hands were like God's healing touch
to show Jesus Christ reaching out
as he loved her so much.

I watched the priest placing oil
on her forehead and hands.
Mum told me that oil shows God's Spirit.
But I couldn't understand.

My grandmother opened her eyes
as the priest began to pray
for healing; easing her suffering
and to take her sins away.

Then, we all said the Lord's Prayer
and I knew she could hear.
She smiled a little smile
as if she knew that God was near.

The priest gave her communion.
It was a very special time.
I remembered that this was Jesus
and no longer bread and wine.

As she looked up at the priest
very pale and frail and white
I knew that God was with her
and that we were in HIS light.

Copyright Susannah White

TASKS
a)   Describe two ways in which you think the Sacrament of the Sick has helped this person.
b)   How do you think it may have helped the family?

6. Christianity & Other Faiths

Nostra Aetate

"All nations are one community and have one origin, because God caused the whole human race to dwell on the face of the earth. They also have one final end, God, whose providence, manifestation of goodness and plans for salvation are extended to all" (para 1).

"The Catholic Church rejects nothing of those things which are true and holy in these religions. It regards with respect those ways of acting and living and those precepts and teachings which, though often at variance with what it holds and expounds, frequently reflect a ray of truth which enlightens everyone.... It therefore calls upon all its sons and daughters with prudence and charity, through dialogue and co-operation with the followers of other religions, bearing witness to the Christian faith and way of life, to recognise, preserve and promote those spiritual and moral good things as well as the socio-cultural values which are to be found among them." (para. 2).

Key Learning objectives

Attainment Targets 1: Learning *about* the Catholic faith.
Attainment Targets 2: Learning *from* the Catholic faith.

*   Know how Christianity continues to spread throughout the world.
    o   Reflect on the reasons for the spread of Catholic Christianity in many parts of the world.

*   Be familiar with the experiences of some of the great missionaries.
    o   Reflect on what we can learn from them.

*   Know what the Catholic Church teaches about other Faiths
    o   Think of ways in which we can work with young people of other Faiths

*   Know about some of the major world religions.
    o   Reflect on some values we share with them.

*   Reflect on some of the bonds of friendship between people of different faiths.
    o   Reflect on what we can learn from them.

*   Know something about the life of Mahatma Gandhi.
    o   Reflect on a personal experience of him.

6 Theological Notes

Christianity and Other Faiths

An appreciation of other faiths and an engagement with them is a constitutive part of Catholic faith – **not** something added on to a Catholic Religious syllabus or some such concession made by a Catholic School to an atmosphere of goodwill. In fact, a Catholic syllabus of Religious Education that omits a study (in both theory and practice) of other faiths is seriously defective.

If the Catholic Church's mission flows from our Catholic belief and self-understanding of "the mystery of the Church", then, in the concrete area of Catholic Religious Education, the approach to other faiths must face squarely and responsibly the fact that it is in the Catholic School and home that children will learn that it is positively possible **not only** for Catholic children to live unabashedly as genuine Catholics who hold firmly, though not uncritically, to their faith in present-day pluralistic society, **but also** for children of other faiths, who frequent our Catholic schools, to live with serene harmony in, and grow up to contribute productively to, our complex and pluralistic society of today.

Consequently it is **imperative** that (a) every Catholic school address the questions raised by the presence in society of persons of other faiths; (b) every Catholic school take on the responsibility of helping <u>all</u> pupils, not only its Catholic students, to integrate faith and life.

It must be clear that **tolerance alone** ("live and let live"!) cannot be the key value to be fostered in the Catholic school's approach to other faiths. For **tolerance alone**, as frequently understood and lived today, implies that all faiths must be relativised – a position which cannot and does not square with the deepest convictions of our Catholic faith. It is the search for, and living of, **positive and genuine harmony** that is the attitude which must animate our entire approach.

Firm Points Of Catholic Faith (never to be played down)

1. There is only one God, the creator of all, Christians and others. God is also the final end of all human beings, since in God alone do they find unending happiness. God's plan of salvation extends to every man and woman without exception. God "wants everyone to be saved and reach the full knowledge of truth" (1 Tim. 2:4).

2. This universal salvific will of God is centred on, and concretised in Jesus Christ, the Son of God, who truly took on human nature "for love of us and for our salvation" (Creed). He is the one mediator between God and human beings, the one and only Saviour of all humanity. "For there is one God, and one Mediator between God and human beings, the man Christ Jesus" (1 Tim. 2:5). "There is no other name under heaven given among human beings, by which we must be saved" (Acts 4:12).

3. All who are saved – whether Christians, Jews, Muslims or others - are saved through the grace of Christ, even when they do not expressly know this or consciously accept Christ as their Saviour. The mystery of salvation reaches out to them, in a way known to God, through the invisible action of the Spirit of Christ [*Gaudium et Spes* (Constitution on the Church in the World Today), n.22; *Dialogue and Proclamation* (Joint Document of Pontifical Council for Interreligious Dialogue and Congregation for the Evangelisation of Peoples), n. 29].

4. There are elements of truth and goodness in other religions; yet deep and great respect for these other faiths does not take away from the need, always with prudence and charity, to proclaim Christ to their followers.

Whatever is good in the minds and hearts of human beings, whatever good lies latent in the religious practices and cultures of diverse peoples, is deeply respected by the Catholic Church, and sought to be completed (healed, ennobled and perfected to the glory of God and the full happiness of these human beings) in and by Christ Jesus.

For reference purposes, here are some key documents relating to the Church and its relationship to other Faiths:

Church Documents

a) Pertinent Documents of Vatican II

1. **Declaration on the Relationship of the Church to Non-Christian Religions** (*Nostra Aetate – NA*) , nn. 1,2,3,4,5 - [nn. 2,3,4 give brief but relevant descriptions of Hinduism, Buddhism, Islam, Judaism].
2. **Dogmatic Constitution on the Church** (*Lumen Gentium – LG*), nn. 13,16,17 - [esp. n. 16].
3. **Decree on the Church's Missionary Activity** (*Ad Gentes – AG*), nn. 3,7,11,22 - [esp. n. 11].
4. **Pastoral Constitution on the Church in the Modern World** (*Gaudium et Spes – GS*), nn. 22,42,45,76,92 - [esp. n. 22].
5. **Declaration on Religious Freedom** (*Dignitatis Humanae*), nn. 1,2,3 - [esp. n. 2: "The truth cannot impose itself except by virtue of its own truth, as it wins over the mind with both gentleness and power"].

b) Papal Documents

1. Pope Paul VI

+ *"Ecclesiam Suam"* – Pope Paul's first encyclical letter of 6th August 1964, esp. its Third Part on "Dialogue", nn. 65-69; 70; 71-77; 78-80; 81-82; 83-86; 87-88; 94-96; 97-98; 107-108.
+ *"Evangelii Nuntiandi"* – Apostolic Exhortation of 8th December 1975 after the Synod of Bishops on "Evangelisation", esp. its nn. 53; 78-79.

2. Pope John Paul II

+ *"Redemptor Hominis"* - Pope John Paul's first encyclical letter of 4th March 1979, esp. its n. 6.
+ *"Dominum et Vivificantem"* – encyclical of 18th May 1986, esp. its n. 53: "... The Second

Vatican Council, centred primarily on the theme of the Church, reminds us of the Holy Spirit's activity also 'outside' the visible body of the Church. The Council speaks precisely of "all people of goodwill in whose hearts grace works in an unseen way. For since Christ died for all, and since the ultimate vocation of human beings is in fact one and divine, we ought to believe that the Holy Spirit, in a manner known only to God, offers to every human being the possibility of being associated with this paschal mystery (*GS* 22)".

+ "***Redemptoris Missio***" – encyclical of 7th December 1990, esp. its n. 28.

+ "***Catechism of the Catholic Church – CCC***" – approved by Pope John Paul II on 25th June 1992, and published on 11th October 1992, esp. its nn. 839-845 (on "The Church and Other Religions") and nn. 27, 28 and 39 (on "The Human Quest for God").

+ "***Tertio Millenio Adveniente***" – Apostolic Letter of 10th November 1994 on the approaching Third Millenium, esp. its nn. 6,19,38,46 and **particularly 52.**

c) Documents of Roman Dicasteries

+ "***The Attitude of the Church towards Other Religions – Reflections and Orientations on Dialogue and Mission***" (Document of the Secretariat for Non-Christians, 10th May 1984).

+ "***Dialogue and Proclamation – Reflections and Orientations on Interreligious Dialogue and the Proclamation of the Gospel of Jesus Christ***" (Joint Document of the Pontifical Council for Interreligious Dialogue and the Congregation for the Evangelisation of Peoples, 19th May 1991), esp. its nn. 14, <u>15</u>, 16, 17, <u>37</u>.

Clear Guidelines For Our Approach

1. The ultimate unity of the entire human family in its origin and destiny is a **first absolute,** the common fundamental element and common root of all religions (see *Nostra Aetate*, n.1).

2. A positive appreciation of the strengths of other faiths, seeking in them the signs of God's presence – whether in Hinduism or Buddhism, Islam or Judaism (see *NA*, n. 2 for such key characteristics of major world religions). Long rooted in tradition is a Christian conviction of the "seeds of the Word" present in all religions. Identifying such "seeds" can help in training for a common collaborative approach of the various faiths to respond to the needs of today's world.

3. The gift of God's grace is **absolutely free and universal.** It is beyond our human control. The path of divine grace is mysterious - we cannot grasp how God deals with human beings in their real, concrete, existential conditions and situations. God **has spoken and continues to speak** in a **variety of ways.**

4. Besides, we must acknowledge that there is **a variety of ways in which human beings respond to God and God's grace** in their concrete existential situations, including their religious adherence. Religions are responses made to the human encounter with the mystery of God.

5. The religious traditions of humanity are significant and positive elements in the economy of God's design of salvation. Therefore, in our approach to, and dialogue with, other faiths we are in a "dialogue of salvation". "Interreligious dialogue", said Pope John Paul II in an important address to the *Pontifical Council for Interreligious Dialogue* on 13th November 1992, "is always, at its deepest level, a dialogue of salvation because it seeks to discern, to clarify and understand better the signs of the age-long dialogue which God maintains with humanity."

6. God's Holy Spirit has been at work in all religious traditions. Hence an approach to, and dialogue with, other faiths is a journeying to discern the Spirit's paths and the direction of grace in these faiths. It is, consequently, a **spiritual act**: such journeying can only be done, if we are open to God's Spirit and alert to the Spirit's voice and call.

7. It is quite clear that such an approach on our part can never be in opposition to our faith-gifted convictions and experience of the centrality of the mystery of Jesus Christ and of God's saving power in Jesus Christ's life, teaching, death and resurrection. It is these experiences and convictions that we share with our sisters and brothers of other faiths, with prudence and charity, in ways that do not constitute an exclusion of their religious experiences.

8. However, it must be remembered that these unshakable convictions and claims about Christ as the unique fulfilment of God's search for human beings have come to human individuals and groups in the concrete experience of their history and their experiences. And this applies as well to our conviction of Christ as the unique fulfilment of our human search for God.

   It is a fact of history – **reality** – that these, our own Christian and Catholic convictions and claims, are obscured and rendered less credible by the life example of Christians and Catholics. We must be deeply sensitive to our profound failure to live the faith we proclaim, harbouring no sense of superiority to anyone, but rather confessing our failings and seeking pardon – as Pope John Paul II did publicly on the occasion of the Jubilee Year 2000 (see his Apostolic Letter *Tertio Millenio Adveniente*, paragraphs 33 and 36, and his *Crossing The Threshold Of Hope*, pp. 79-80).

Practical Suggestions

Since, for us Christians, Christ is the fulfilment, both of God's search for us human beings and our search as human beings for God, we could take these two major approaches.

(A) How do the different faiths experience God's saving action?
     [We know that, in Christianity, we have our understanding of God's saving action in Christ.]

A sharing of experiences in the first place can then lead to what we have earlier termed the positive appreciation of the experiences of other faiths.

(B)   Since "religions" are the human responses to God's search for human beings, the various faiths express these experiences in their "quest for God".

In facing fundamental life-questions great help can be found in *NA* 1 (final paragraph); also in *GS* 4 ("Hope and Anguish"), and *Gaudium et Spes* 10 ("The Human Person's Deeper Questionings").

How do the different faiths express their experiences in facing these life-questions?

Again here, a **sharing of experiences** can then lead to the positive appreciation of the experiences of other faiths.

How do the different faiths reflect on the mystery of creation?

How do the different faiths reflect on the "environment" in which human beings live?

How do they reflect on the responsibility of human beings for their "environment"? Questions of "ecology"…?

In facing the relationship between religious faith and commitment to society:

A **sharing of experiences** on how to face the key social issues of today's world:
peace, justice, promotion of positive attitudes towards human life – especially its most vulnerable moments of birth and death – building up human community, society, solidarity.

To prepare for joint action in common with other faiths on these key social issues:

The basis for joint action: a shared appraisal of what needs to be done and how to approach the task. Admittedly, at the level of school children, such joint action is fairly limited in scope; but, if a school is linked to a local community through its teachers and parents, children can be amazingly creative in reaching out to those in need.

The Personal Dimension of Religious Education:

Even in Religious Education classes we are aiming at contributing to the **personal** life of faith of each pupil, as we are when we approach other faiths. For, in this approach, we expect to learn something of God's ways and be enriched by them **personally**.

Such an aim is more effectively achieved by some **personal experiences** of the **life** and **practices** of a faith than by a mere abstract study of the same.

For this, **in practice**, our Catholic schools would do well to organise:

(1) visits to centres of other faiths; (2) return visits to Catholic schools and churches.

In such visits, the accent could be placed on **ways of personal prayer or worship**, as also **of prayer and worship in common;** also on **other religious and devotional practices.**

The whole point is to emphasise the dimension of **experience sharing**, not of debate or discussion.

N.B. It is well worth noting that our Catholic school children, with adequate help, are known to be quite capable of undertaking such a responsibility.

Similarly, a Catholic school could regularly invite members and leaders of neighbouring other faith communities to its celebrations and festivities. Return invitations could well be forthcoming, and should not then be turned down.

Conclusion

Our Catholic faith "is a gifted response to the revealed truth – a truth which possesses it, and not a truth which a Catholic can ever pretend to possess. The mature Catholic, therefore, is always a servant of the truth, always standing in need of forgiveness and renewal, seeking to recognise the truth wherever it is to be found, yet fully confident in the mediation of the Church" (The Most Rev. Vincent Nichols, in "The Catholic Church's Mission in Education in a Multi-faith Society" from 'The Birmingham Texts', Education Special, June 1995, p.19).

Herbert Alphonso SJ

Additional Suggestions and Resources

> **Know that Christianity continues to spread throughout the world.**
> **Reflect on the experience and example of St. Paul.**

Starting Point: Invite pupils to think of the most joyful experience of their lives and share it with the person next to them.

Next, ask pupils to try to imagine what they think was the most powerful experience for the apostles. They had left all to follow Jesus. They admired him tremendously; they had witnessed his miracles and they believed he had risen from the dead. But **what** and **when** was the climax of their experience of him? **Pentecost!** It was when they received his **Spirit** that they were truly convinced that Jesus was **GOD**. They remembered all that Jesus had taught them and knew that he would be with them until the end of time.

WS 1 Apostles are overwhelmed by events.

PPP 'St. Paul'. It would be best to show this before reading the text in the Pupil's Book.

DVD Other Resources Folder: Map of Paul's Missionary Journeys.

Assessment Folder for assessment sheet: St. Paul.

http://www.ainglkiss.com/stories/psj.htm Paul and Silas in Jail

Flipcharts: Spread of Christianity.

Discuss the reasons various people give for the growth of Christianity today (Pupil's Book page 106).

Flipchart World Religions: Pie charts showing the percentage of people belonging to religions.

WS 2 Countries with Catholic majority

[Should questions arise regarding why there are so few Catholics in the UK you may want to briefly explain about the Reformation – a module on Christianity in Britain will be in the next book in this series **'The Truth'.**

> ## Be familiar with the experiences of some of the great missionaries.
> ## Reflect on what we can learn from them.

Note: This is an opportunity to make links to all the modules in this book. Highlight how God works through people who open their hearts to Him and have absolute faith in His power to work through human weakness.

It is also an opportunity to develop thinking skills:
Predicting: What would happen if?
Analysing: What is it telling us about …?
Deducing: If it is true then what does it mean for us?
Evaluating: How important are these events/facts/stories for us?

[In the Assessment Folder for this module on the DVD there are ten assessment tasks and three assessment sheets mapped to the Bishops' Conference Levels of Attainment in RE].

Starting Point: PPP St. Francis Xavier. This Power Point is mainly to help lower ability pupils. Others will be able to go straight to the text in the Student's Book.

WS 3 Discuss: *(This could be used for Group Discussion).*
- In 1541, why did it take so long for Francis Xavier to reach India?
- Why do you think he went first to the very poor to spread the Gospel?
- He met with many difficulties. Why do you think he did not give up?
- When you are doing something important and meet with difficulties, what do you do?
- We are told he baptised tens of thousands of people. How do you think he managed to do this? *(Think about the experience of St. Paul).*
- Why do you think he wanted to go to Japan?
- What obstacles did he face?
- It appeared in human eyes that he was a failure because there were not many conversions – but find out how many Christians there are in Japan now. Try to find out if there are Jesuits in Japan.
- Francis Xavier did not give up! What did he do next?
- Why do you think he did it?
- Humanly speaking, he did not accomplish anything. But God could see what was in his heart. What do you think was the 'long-term' outcome?

WS 4 St. Francis Xavier (Guided thinking – success & disappointments.)

Martyrs of Uganda
Discuss:
- Why do you think King Mwanga was so vehemently opposed to the Christian missionaries?
- What did he forbid the converts to do? Why?
- Think of the courage and determination of the new converts. Reflect on our own situation. What conclusions can we draw? Does complete freedom to be a Christian actually help us? How?
- What surprises you most about these martyrs?

DVD Other Resources Folder: Edel Quinn Biography.
WS 5 Edel Quinn Time-line activity.

DVD Other Resources Folder: Gladys Aylward Biography.
WS 6 Gladys Alyward: Complete the diagram 'Faith, Challenge, Blessing'.

Activities:
1. "Pray as if everything depended on God.
   Act as if everything depended on you." St. Augustine
   a) Read the biography of Gladys Aylward.
   b) To what extent do you think she 'lived out' the words of St. Augustine?
   You are free to use a multi-flow map for your answer.

WS 7: Missionaries I admire (Less able)

WS 8: How missionaries affect others.

Film 'The Inn of the Sixth Happiness' the life of Gladys Aylward is available at HMV on DVD.

> **Know what the Catholic Church teaches about other Faiths.**
> **Think of ways in which we can work with young people of other Faiths.**

Note: Be sure to read for yourself: 'Firm Point of Catholic Faith' (never to be played down) in the Theological Notes page 96.

Starting Point: Ask the pupils to discuss in pairs the reasons why they think it is important to study other faiths and then share with the class. Then they read 'What we believe'. It will help to motivate pupils if you give some time to explaining the importance of having a very good understanding of your own faith.

The 'Points of Catholic Faith' and 'What does the Catholic Church teach about other faiths' will also be held by other Christians.

Notes:
Nostre Aetate: Declaration on the Catholic Church's Relation to non-Christian Religions – document of the Second Vatican Council (1962-1965).

The **Second Vatican Council** (1962-1965) was the twenty-first ecumenical gathering of the Catholic Church. It was a determined effort "to inquire how we (the Church) ought to renew ourselves so that we many be found increasingly faithful to the gospel of Jesus Christ".

Additional Resources DVD ROM: For Activity 2 on page 113 in the Pupil's Book you will find a copy of the Creed. This will help pupils answer the question 'What are the most important beliefs that Catholics hold?'

www.tere.org **Secondary: KS3 Support Material:** click on 'The Church Overseas'; see ICT Section: 'The Pope' fact finding.

Be aware of some of the major world religions.
Reflect on some values we share with them.

WS 9 Starting Point: Pupils complete the first two columns of the KWL chart.

Activities
1. a) Work in pairs. Study the values of different faiths in the Pupil's Book, page 117.
   b) WS 10 'Values we share', Use the double bubble map to compare and contrast these values.

2. Photocopy the following stories from this book pages 109-112.
   - Testing Virtue: Buddhism,
   - Six Blind Men: Hinduism,
   - What Should I Do? Islam (Themes: Sharing, caring, making a sacrifice, friendship),
   - The Good and the Bad: Sikhism (Themes: Kindness, generosity, wisdom).

   a) Choose one story. Write out the most important message in it.
   b) Explain how it may be easy or difficult to live out this message.

PPP World Faiths: Beliefs (Less able).
PPP World Faiths: Worship & Behaviour (Less able).

Activity: Complete the third column of KWL.

WS 11 Jewish worship (Less able).

Assessment Folder for assessment sheets: Other Faiths and Values We Share.

Flipcharts: 'Judaism'; 'Islam'; 'Hinduism'.

Useful websites:
http://atschool.eduweb.co.uk/carolrb/islam/islamintro.html Islam for Children.
http://atschool.eduweb.co.uk/carolrb/judaism/judai1.html Judaism for Children.
http://atschool.eduweb.co.uk/manorlh/hinduism/hindui.html Hindu.

Examples of people or organisations of other faiths who have used their talents and gifts to help those in need: Muhammad Yunus, a Bangladeshi economist who, about 30 years ago, opened a bank to give tiny credit free loans to millions of poor people particularly destitute widows and abandoned wives and beggars to help them build their own small businesses. He won the Nobel Peace Prize in 2006. Try Google search engine 'Peace Prize to Pioneer of Loans to Poor NO Bank Would Touch' and 'Design Your Life – Microfinancing is the New Peace'

Islamic Relief Worldwide (IR) is an international relief and development charity which aims to alleviate the suffering of the world's poorest people.

Other examples:
Ludwik Rajcman, a Jew, who started UNICEF United National International. Children's Emergency Fund – Nobel Prize winner.
Bernard Kouchner, a Jew, who started Medecins sans Frontieres.
Muslim Aid.

Reflect on some of the bonds of friendship between people of different faiths. Reflect on what we can learn from them.

Starting Point: Discuss in pairs: What do we need to build bonds of friendship with people of other faiths?

Study: Memories of Two Boys: Pupil's Book page 119.
  o What can we learn from the friendship of these two boys?
  o Think of the opportunities we have today to build bonds of friendship with young people of different backgrounds, culture, faith, etc.

PPP - Pope John Paul II's Pilgrimage to Israel

Pope John Paul II arrived in Israel on 21 March 2000, for a historic five-day visit, during which he visited the holy places of the three major religions and met Israel's political leaders and Chief Rabbis.

Once there, Pope John Paul II stood before the Western Wall (the holiest place for Jews) and asked forgiveness for past sins of the Christians against the Jews. This was looked upon as the most noble gesture ever done by anyone of another faith.

Discuss: The Rabbi & the Cardinal

- o How easy or difficult is it for us to get to know young people of other faiths?
- o Who has friends of another faith? Encourage pupils to talk about what they can do together.
- o What can we do to build bonds of friendship with young people of other faiths? Think of something you can do as a class or as an individual.
- o What can we learn from the Chief Rabbi's decision not to take part in the funeral at Westminster Cathedral – but to find another way to honour the memory of his friend?

PPP Annalena Tonelli

WS 12 Annalena Tonelli

Other Resources Folder: Annalena Tonelli Biography.

Work in pairs. Very few people have heard of Annalena Tonelli. Plan to make her known to the whole school. Try to find out more about her on the Internet

Additional Activities

1. **Catholic Father – Muslim Mother** Pupil's Book page 121.
   a) Identify the important beliefs in this story.
   b) Why did Renato want to convert his mother?
   c) What did Renato have to learn?
   d) Was he right? Give reasons for your answer.

Starting Point:

Gandhi – A True Story: Pupils could benefit from hearing this true story read by an adult and time allowed for reflection on it before working on it in their own textbook.

Flipcharts: 'Gandhi'

Additional resources: relevant video clip:

Put into Google: American Rhetoric: Movie Speeches G-L.

Then click on **Mr. & Mrs. Gandhi address to the people** of India.

[Also available: Gandhi to British Authorities "It is time you left" Gandhi's address to Indian National Congress, Gandhi advocates policy of Non Violence]

http://myhero.com/myhero/heroasp?hero=gandhi Peacemaker Hero: Mohandas K. Gandhi.

http://www.uni.edu/gai/India_Lesson_Plans?Ghandhis_Story.htm Gandhi's Story.

http://mkgandhi-sarvodaya.org/story_of_gandhi.htm The Story of Gandhi.

http://mkgandhi-sarvodaya.org/story.htm Inspiring Stories from Gandhi's Life.

http://mkgandhi-sarvodaya.org/story.htm   Non-Violent Resistance to Injustice; All Humans are Equal; Civil Disobedience; Gandhi's Visit to England.

Poem
Six Blind Men And The Elephant
(A Hindu Parable)

It was six men of Indostan
To learning much inclined
Who went to see the Elephant
(Though all of them were blind)
That each by observation
Might satisfy his mind.

The first approached the Elephant
And happening to fall
Against his broad sturdy side
At once began to bawl:
"God bless me! But the Elephant
Is very like a wall!"

The second feeling of the tusk
Cried, "Ho!   What have we here,
So very round and smooth and sharp?
To me tis mighty clear
This wonder of an Elephant
Is very like a spear!"

The third approached the animal
And happening to take
The squirming trunk with his hands,
That boldly up he spake:
"I see," quoth he, "the Elephant
Is very like a snake!"

The fourth reached out an eager hand
And felt about the knee
"What most this wondrous beast is like
Is mighty plain," quoth he;
"Tis clear enough the Elephant

Is very like a tree!"

The fifth, who chanced to touch the ear,
Said: "E'en the blindest man
Can tell what this resembles most;
Deny the fact who can,
This marvel of an Elephant
Is very like a fan!"

The sixth no sooner had begun
About the beast to grope,
Than, seizing on the swinging tail
That fell within his scope.
"I see," quoth he, "the Elephant
Is very like a rope!"

And so the men of Indostan
Disputed loud and long,
Each in his own opinion
Exceeding stiff and strong
Though each was partly in the right
And all were in the wrong!

MORAL

So oft in theologic wars
The disputants, I ween
Rail on in utter ignorance
Of what each other mean
And prate about an Elephant
Not one of them has seen.

By John Godfrey Saxe (1816-1887)

Testing Virtue
A Buddhist Story

Once upon a time, when King Brahmadatta was reigning in Benares, the Bodhisatta was his family priest, a wise and learned man who strove to live a faultless life, intent on observing faithfully the five moral virtues.* The king honoured the Bodhisatta above all other brahmans.

Now it came about that the Bodhisatta began to wonder whether the king treated him with honour because of his high moral conduct in respect of his observation of the moral virtues or was the honour due to his great learning and wisdom? The Bodhisatta decided to test which was higher - moral conduct or learning.

So one day he took a coin from a money-lender's counter. The money-lender said nothing because of the Bodhisatta's respected status. The next day he again took a coin from the counter of the money lender. Again the money-lender said nothing because of the great respect in which the Bodhisatta was held. The following day a third coin was taken. The money-lender had had enough. He seized the Bodhisatta, bound him and brought him before the king.

"What has my respected Bodhissata done?" asked the king.
"Respected Bodhissata!" spluttered the money-lender. "This man is a pilfering thief. He has stolen my property."
"Is this really true, Brahman?" The king could not believe what he was hearing.
"Your Majesty," replied the Bodhissata, "I do not steal property. But I was in doubt which was greater, observing the moral virtues or learning. So to test which of these is greater I took a coin three times from the money-lender's counter. This is why I stand before you now, bound and accused of theft. Now I know that moral behaviour through living according to the virtues is greater than learning."

And he spoke these lines:
"I had a doubt: Is virtue better? Is learning better?
I have no doubt: Virtue is better than learning.
Birth is vain and caste, virtue itself is quite the highest.
No worth exists in learning unless refined by virtue."

*The Five Virtues are:
  No violence – reverence for all life.
  No one must steal – respect the property of others.
  No one must lie – do not deceive but speak honestly and truthfully.
  Respect fellow men and women – be conscious and loving in relationships.
  Do not drink alcohol or take drugs – take proper care of body and mind.

A Buddhist Story, adapted from Jataka Stories No. 362, Vol 111 by Angela Edwards
Published with permission from the Buddhist Society.

The Good and the Bad

Guru Nanak travelled far and wide teaching people the right way to live.

Once he was travelling through Bengal in India with his friends Bhai Bala and Bhai Mardana. They walked from village to village on foot and were often hungry and tired when they arrived.

One night, they could travel no further and they stopped at a village to stay for the night. They asked some people whether they could give them a bed and some food. The villagers rudely replied, "Go away we do not care for strangers here".

They asked many other villagers and over and over they received the same reply. Finally, they lay down outside and went to sleep, cold and hungry.

The next morning they got up early, sang hymns and prayed to God. Guru Nanak said, "May these people stay in this village for ever". Then they set off on their journey. Bhai Mardana thought about what Guru Nanak had said and felt upset – but he couldn't understand why the Guru had blessed such rude and unkind people. But he didn't say anything.

At the end of the day, they reached another village. The people of that village were just the opposite – they welcomed everyone who arrived there and were kind to the Guru and his friends. They served them food with loving care and offered them comfortable beds for the night.

In the morning, Guru Nanak said, "Let us pray", and they prayed for the good of all. After the prayer Guru Nanak said, "May the people of this village scatter". Mardana felt upset again. What did the Guru mean? This time he said to Guru Nanak, "Guru, I don't understand your wishes. You wish the unkind to stay happily in one place. It seems as if you are cursing the good and blessing the bad!"

Guru Nanak replied, "Listen to me, dear Mardana. I did not curse the good people, rather I wish that they may scatter and live in other parts of the world. Wherever they go they will make people good by their example. If there are more good people then the world will be a happier place. The other people are good for nothing! They will make other people rude and unkind wherever they go, so it is better if they stay in their own village". Mardana was no longer upset. He realised what the Guru meant. If we are kind and gentle to others it will please the Lord.

Adapted from: Guru Nanak for Children by GS Sidhu, GS Sivia and Kirpal Sing.
Published with permission of the Sikh Missionary Society.

What should I do?

Ahmed was a Muslim. All his life he had heard and read of the city of Makkah, where the beloved Prophet was born and to which Muslims longed to go on pilgrimage. He had joined in the farewell celebrations for those making the journey. He had read books, looked at photographs. One day, one day, he would make that exciting journey!

The years passed, he married and had children. Although he longed to visit Makkah he knew that first he must make sure that his family was provided for. The pilgrimage cost such a lot of money and he could not leave his wife to struggle with three small children and an elderly mother-in-law. God would want him to put his family first, before his own wishes and his friends who would want him to travel with them. But one day, one day ….

At last, the day arrived. He could afford to pay for the journey without hardship to his family. Everyone helped him prepare for this exciting visit. Fellow Muslims at the mosque shared his happiness and shared their memories with him.

At last the great day arrived. After morning prayers at the mosque he went to say good-bye to his friend Mushtaq whom he had not seen for a few weeks. He had forgotten that he had lost his job and was unemployed. Mushtaq hesitated before asking him into the house. Why? At last Mushtaq explained that money was scarce – after buying the children shoes there has hardly been any money for food….

Returning home Ahmed began to feel uneasy. If he gave his pilgrimage money to Mushtaq he would be able to feed and clothe his family. He talked with his wife – he had so much wanted to make the pilgrimage but …. They agreed, the money should be given to his friend. Friends belong to each other, he must share what he had.

Ahmed's friends thought they had missed him at the airport. He must have caught an earlier plane. Ahmed shared the festival of Eid-ul-Adha with his family and friends at home. Days passed.

The travellers returned, proud, happy, excited, longing to share their experiences with their fellow Muslims.

"Was it really so wonderful?" Ahmed asked, wistfully.
"Of course", they replied. "But you know it was, we saw you there."

RE Today Spring 1992 Published by CEM